F//TPRINTS
DISCOVERING LOCAL HISTORY

General Editor: Roger Whiting

GW01393121

THE COUNTRYSIDE

ROGER WHITING

Formerly Head of History, King's School, Gloucester

TIMOTHY LOMAS and MICHAEL WISE

Ludlow School

Stanley Thornes (Publishers) Ltd

First published in 1987 by:
Stanley Thornes (Publishers) Ltd
Old Station Drive
Leckhampton
CHELTENHAM GL53 0DN
England

British Library Cataloguing in Publication Data

Footprints.
    Countryside
    1.   Great Britain — History, Local
    I.   Whiting, Roger
    941   DA30

    ISBN 0-85950-686-X

Cover illustration: Weston, near Spalding, reproduced by kind
permission of Aerofilms Ltd.

Typeset by Tech-Set, Gateshead, Tyne & Wear
Printed and bound in Great Britain by Ebenezer Baylis & Son,
Worcester

Contents

WARNING. REMEMBER TO GET PERMISSION FROM THE OWNERS OF ANY PRIVATE LAND, OR BUILDINGS, YOU WANT TO ENTER DURING YOUR RESEARCH.

Acknowledgements

The authors and publishers are grateful to the following for supplying and giving permission to reproduce prints and artwork:

Aerofilms Ltd, pp. 9, 10, 17 (bottom left)
Barnaby's Picture Library, p. 14
BBC Hulton Picture Library, p. 20
Mrs R.F. Bidgood, p. 23 (top)
Cambridge University Collection, Crown Copyright Reserved, p. 13
Cornwall Archaeological Society, p. 16 (top)
David & Charles Publishers Ltd, pp. 5, 12 (top), 16 (bottom), 26 (bottom), 28
Farmers Weekly Picture Library, p. 25
Gloucestershire County Record Office, document deposited in the Record Office by Mrs Clifford of Frampton (GRO ref. D149), p. 8; documents from the Robert Hughes papers (GRO ref. D245), pp. 37, 38, 39; and pp. 40, 41
Trustees of the Goodwood Collections, with acknowledgements to the West Sussex Record Office and the County Archivist, p. 4
Mr M. Greenhalgh, Langley Park Boys' School, Beckenham, p. 6
Mr J.E. Manners, p. 22 (bottom)
The Mansell Collection, pp. 31, 43
Mr J.W.G. Musty, p. 17 (right)
Nottinghamshire Leisure Services (Libraries) Department, p. 1
Dr J.E.C. Peters, pp. 15, 22 (top left and top right), 29 (right)
Routledge & Kegan Paul Ltd, p. 26 (top)
Mr Philip Sauvain, pp. 2, 19
University of Reading, Institute of Agricultural History and Museum of English Rural Life, pp. 21, 27
Weald & Downland Open Air Museum, pp. 23 (bottom), 24 (top)
Mr J.B. Weller, *History of the Farmstead*, p. 29 (left)
Welsh Folk Museum, p. 24 (bottom)
Mr Reece Winstone, p. 17 (top left)

All other prints are reproduced by kind permission of the authors.

We are also grateful to the following for additional material:

King's School, Gloucester, and Langley Park Boys' School, Beckenham, for reference to their project work
Norman Wills's *Woad in the Fens*, which quotes an interview with Walter Booth of Skirbeck

And all those schools who responded to a letter from the publishers inviting information about their local history work – and whose material was helpful in providing general background for the series.

1 Footprints of the Past

Sometimes history seems to be something which happens somewhere else and affects only other people. That may be true of wars and the rise and fall of governments, but there is just as much history on your *doorstep*. In fact the effect of warfare and the changing of governments may well have caused big changes in your locality. Your comprehensive school may well have been a grammar or secondary modern school a few years ago. The street it faces on to may refer to a time when your locality was part of the defence complex needed in times of rebellion or invasion, such as *Castle Street*, to take a random example. Your own home may have a history, or, if it is a new one, the estate on which it stands may well have a tale to tell. Odd curves in country roads or hump lines across fields were once put there for a purpose. The alterations to the local church or mill reflect the changes they had to face up to in bygone days. There is nothing to stop you becoming a *historian-detective* to find out what the story is behind so much that is around you. This series of booklets aims to equip you for this exciting and rewarding task.

The countryside we see today is the result of centuries of use. How have people used it? Why did they use it in those ways? Can you find signs of places no longer used, such as medieval villages? What can you work out from the existing farm buildings you see around the countryside? Some of the answers you will find by studying documents, and others by going out on the site with a measuring tape, notebook and camera.

Does all this sound rather difficult? This booklet will give you examples of what you can find for yourself, and where to find them. You will then be able to go to your local record office, library or museum, knowing what kind of things to ask for. You will also know what to look for in the countryside itself. You may know how other people have tackled similar problems and found exciting evidence in all sorts of ways.

Any historian-detective will want to find out:

(a) What signs are there that things have changed very little? Experts call this *continuity*, that is, things continuing roughly the same down the ages.

(b) What *changes* have occurred, and why?

All history is made up of a combination of continuity and change. It is fascinating to find out why some things change very little, if at all, while others change a lot.

Chapter 2 is an introduction to the different kinds of evidence you can search for. Chapter 3 gives further details on documents, before Chapter 4 takes you out 'on site'. Other chapters will give you further information. Chapter 7 shows how two schools tackled research in different ways. Then you will be ready to do your own research.

2 Looking at the Countryside

As you glance from the window of a car or a train, you may spot unusual ground shapes or buildings and wonder what they are. Why did people develop the land in that way, and construct buildings just like that? If you are walking in the countryside you will get even closer to such features. We all depend on the produce of the land, and it is well worth finding out how our ancestors obtained that produce. What kinds of evidence will you need to examine to answer these questions? Here is a brief summary. We will look at these in more detail in the chapters that follow.

(a) *On the ground* You will probably find mounds, ditches, regular dips and banks across fields, rectangular markings, old buildings now no longer used, old buildings adapted to new uses, and so on. These can give you a lot of clues about how the land was used. See Chapters 4 and 7.

(b) *Tools and machines* Museums contain a large number of farm tools (or 'implements') and machines. Close examination of them will help us to understand how farming was done in the past. Chapter 5 talks briefly about these and includes a list of helpful books.

(c) *Documents* There is a great range of documents you can look at: maps, plans, account books, letters, posters, farm implement catalogues, ancient books, old magazines, wills and inventories, to name but a few. See Chapters 3 and 7.

(d) *Oral history* Interviewing old people about how things were done in their time is often exciting as they can really bring a subject to life. The only problem is that they cannot take us back beyond the early days of their own lifetimes, unless they can remember what their parents and grandparents told them years ago. See Chapter 6.

FURTHER READING

Toulson, S. *Discovering Farm Museums and Farm Parks* (Shire Publications, 1977)

3 Finding and Using Documents

Documents are vital for historical research and you should look in your local county record office, museum or library for the kinds of document dealt with in this section.

COUNTY RECORD OFFICES

Each county has a record office, usually in the county town, where all kinds of old (and quite new) records are kept. Anyone is allowed to do research in these offices. You will find the staff helpful. Allow plenty of time when you first go there, as the documents need to be found in the indexes and then brought up from the vaults. Take a notebook and a pencil – you will not be allowed to use a pen. The staff will help you with some difficult handwriting, but they cannot read it all for you as they are far too busy!

MAPS

STUDYING MAPS
Consider these questions. Are the fields curved or square? How do they relate to the shape of the roads? If both are curved, they were probably enclosed early on; while square fields and straight roads suggest later enclosure, done more mathematically. Is there any evidence of earlier farming methods? What differences are there between the details on old and new maps?

TITHE MAPS
These refer to the *tithe*, a tax amounting to one-tenth of agricultural produce, usually paid by local landowners to the parish priest as part of his income. But it was sometimes paid to another person who had acquired the right to the tithes. For many years the tithe was paid in the form of crops which were then stored in a tithe barn. It only became a cash tax in the nineteenth century.

A sorting out of the system in 1836 led to a survey of the land, and as part of this survey tithe maps of 12–25 in. to the mile were drawn. They are less detailed than the large-scale Ordnance Survey maps (see page 5), but they should have a full *schedule*, or written explanation,

to go with them. Barns, stables, yards and so on are usually given, and the tithe details may include the crops growing at the time. You will have to get someone to help you trace the right *tithe award* (settlement) to go with the map and its schedule. Advice on this can be found in *Local History, A Handbook for Beginners* by P. Rider (Batsford, 1983).

ENCLOSURE AWARD MAPS
These were made in the eighteenth and early nineteenth centuries. When villages replaced their old field patterns with newer ones, which were often smaller and enclosed by a hedge or ditch, a map was frequently needed. One map showing ownership of the existing strips, and another showing who would own the new farms, were done for each village (see the section on Land Enclosure on page 12 and the maps of Cold Aston on pages 40–1). A comparison of tithe and enclosure maps for the same village can tell you a lot about farming changes. An on-site check will show whether there has been change or continuity *since* the time of enclosure.

RAILWAY COMPANIES' PLANNING MAPS
These were done when getting permission to construct new lines before about 1880. They show how a line would have affected the land it was to go through. These maps were submitted to the Quarter Sessions meetings of magistrates. It does not matter if the line was never built; the maps are still useful. So check in your local record office to see if there are any.

COUNTY MAPS
A number of different county maps were done for sale, but they often show little of real value. C. & J. Greenwood's county 1 inch series of the 1820s may help a bit.

PRIVATE ESTATE MAPS
These will show quite a lot of details, such as owners of fields, streams, pounds (pens for holding lost or confiscated livestock), wastelands, lanes and so on.

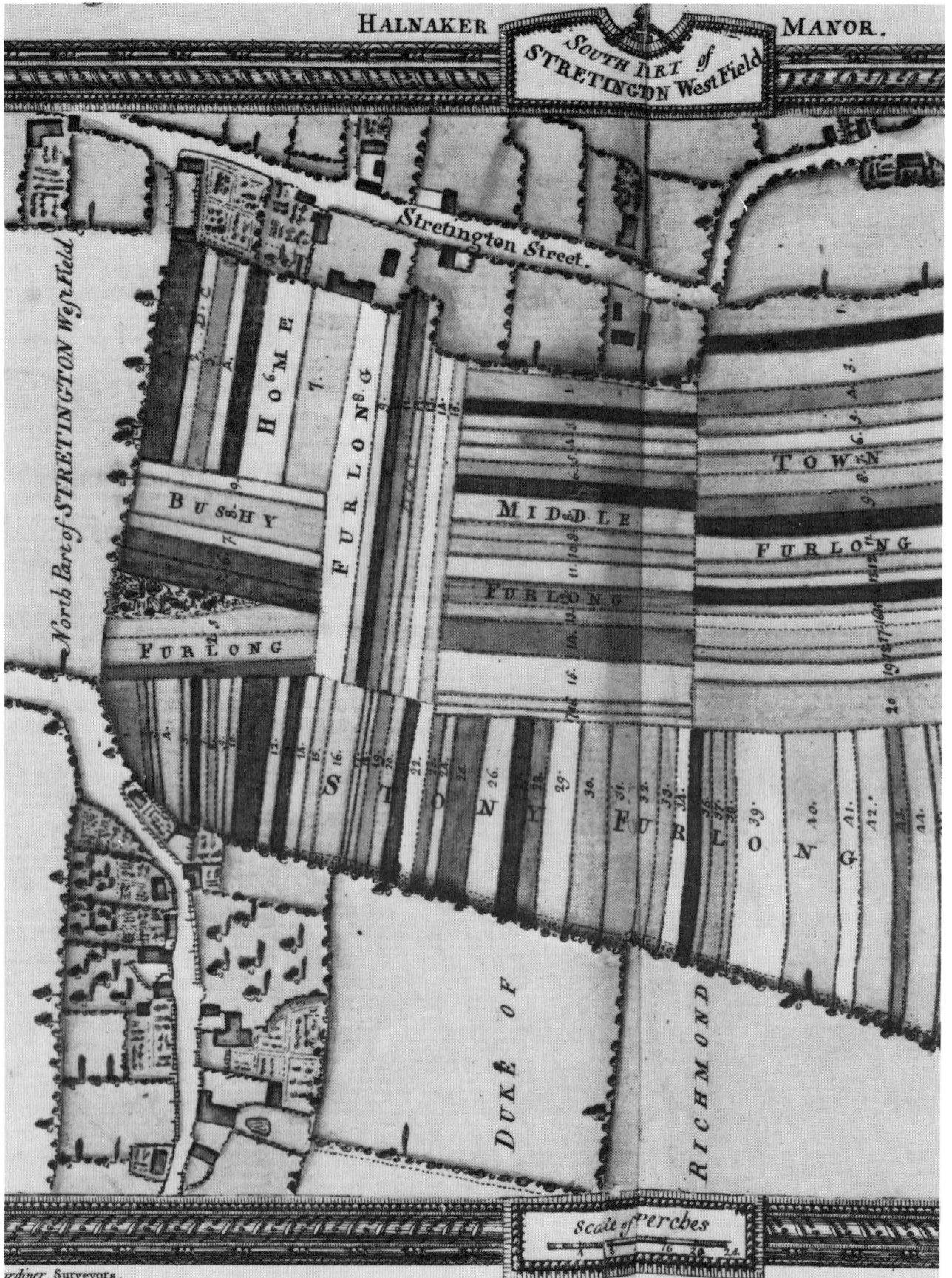

HALNAKER

SOUTH PART of
STRETINGTON WestField

MANOR.

Stretington Street.

North Part of STRETINGTON West Field

HOME

BUSHY

FURLONG

FURLONG

MIDDLE

FURLONG

STONY

FURLONG

TOWN

FURLONG

DUKE OF

RICHMOND

Scale of Perches

rdiner, Surveyors.

Private Estate Map of Stretington, Sussex, 1781. Find the village street and the open fields.

LARGE-SCALE ORDNANCE SURVEY (O.S.) MAPS

These will locate farms and their surroundings. The local library, museum or record office may have earlier editions of the map you need. Ordnance Survey work began in Kent, Surrey and Sussex in the 1790s, so that preparations could be made to fight off any French invasion. This led on to the 'Old Series' of 1 in. to the mile maps, which were completed by 1870. (One inch equals about 2.54 cm.) The publishers David & Charles Ltd have recently republished the Old Series maps. Two in. to the mile engravings from which the 1 in. maps were done are available in photostat form from the Map Room of the British Museum, or from the National Library of Wales. From the 1870s onwards O.S. produced 6 in. and 25 in. to the mile maps. The 25 in. maps give outlines of buildings, field boundaries and acreages, while the 6 in. ones will cover a whole parish.

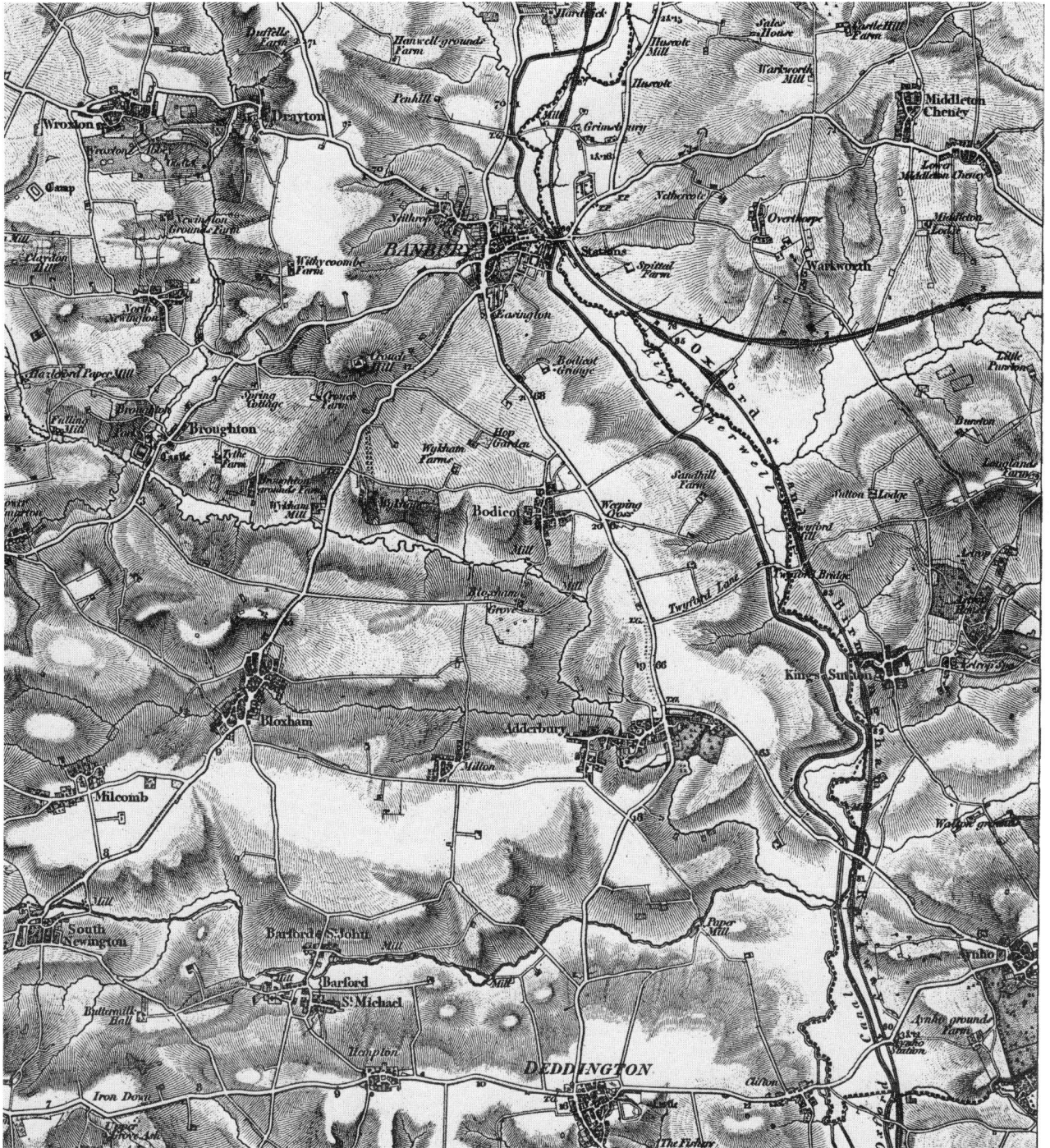

Part of a reprinted Old Series map of 1833, showing the area of North Oxfordshire around Banbury

DOMESDAY SURVEY

The Domesday survey of 1086 is an excellent starting point for your work on a particular piece of countryside. Recently the publishers Phillimore & Co., Chichester, have published the *Domesday Book* in county volumes, with the Latin text on one page and the clear English translation on the facing page. Summaries and maps are included too. Langley Park School for Boys, Beckenham, has looked at the *Domesday Book* report on Bromley. Below is a sample of the material they worked on. To understand it you will need to know these terms:

> Borderer: *person dwelling on the border of the land*
> Carucate: *amount of land ploughed by one ox in one year (120 acres)*
> Demesne: *lord's own land used solely by him*
> Hundred: *originally area containing 100 houses*
> Pannage: *grazing area as given by the king*
> Suling: *about 120 acres*
> Villein: *peasant farmer working at his lord's command*
> Yields: *pays up in taxes*

"In Bromley <u>hundred</u> the same bishop of Rochester holds Bromley. It was taxed at six <u>sulings</u> in the time of Edward the Confessor, and now at three. The arable land is 13 <u>carucates</u>. In <u>demesne</u> there are 2 <u>carucates</u>, and 30 <u>villeins</u>, with 26 <u>borderers</u> having 11 <u>carucates</u>. There is one mill of 4 shillings, and 2 acres of meadow. Wood for the <u>pannage</u> of 100 hogs. In the time of King of Edward the Confessor, and afterwards, it was worth 12 pounds and 10 shillings (£12.50), now 18 pounds, and yet it <u>yields</u> 21 pounds, all but 2 shillings."

NAMES

Field, street and pub names can be helpful. Incidentally, if you live in a town, you may be surprised to find how a street map gives information about the farming that once went on in what is now a housing estate! Blackpool's map has Hayfield, Little Acre, Longfield, Old Meadow, Southfield, Westfield and Tithe Barn marked on it. Here are some examples of place-name endings which may give us clues: *bourne* – brook; *burgh* – fort; *den* – pasture ground or shelter; *ham* – homestead or village; *ley* – open ground, wood; *stead* – place; *stoke* – place; *thorpe* – settlement; *thwaite* – meadow or clearing; *ton* – enclosure, village; *wick* – dairy farm or settlement in general.

Look up public houses in the *Yellow Pages*. Find where such pubs as the Plough, the Glebe Hotel, the Jolly Thresher, the Wheelwright's Arms, etc. are to be found.

COURT CASES

Ludlow School in Shropshire made use of *court rolls* (lists of land holdings, etc., of a manorial court). For example:

John Jenkinson of Billingham received his land in good condition 3 years ago but has since neglected it. He has not manured his lands at all preferring to sell his manure. His lands have thus got into a dreadful state and weeds and other horrible things have spread from his lands onto those of his neighbour

(1365)

To stop people stealing other people's land the prior insists that boundary stones called merestones shall be put in to separate people's strips

(1370)

7 tenants are fined 6d each because they have ploughed up for their own land the pathways between the strips known as balks

(1370)

The Domesday Book *for Bromley*

INVENTORIES

These are lists of property made either when someone died (so that the directions in a will could be carried out) or when a farm was sold. Below is a list from Hunt Farm, Gloucestershire, made in 1831, when the farm was sold on the owner's death. The farm produced butter, cheese, beer and cider. There were then 114 acres of arable (ploughing) land (including 40 acres of wheat, 20 acres of beans, 9 acres of peas, 17 acres of turnips, and 6 acres of barley) and 130 acres of pasture. If you can find several inventories or sale lists for the same farm you will be able to learn a lot of its history.

COWS	£	s	d
12 cows in/with calf	147	15	0
11 3-yr-old cows	137	15	0
6 2-yr-old cows	37	15	0
1 3-yr-old bull	10	0	0
1 2-yr-old bull	3	17	2
1 1-yr-old bull	5	15	0
HAY			
10 tons in stack yard	29	8	0
10 tons in rick yard	17	10	0
10 tons in orchard	4	10	0
IMPLEMENTS [small part of whole list]			
3 wagons	27	5	0
1 light wagon with iron arms	3	17	0
2 long narrow-wheeled carts	7	9	0
4 long ploughs	4	5	0
1 winnowing machine	4	0	0
2 wagon ropes	1	3	6
1 crosscut & handsaw		11	6
1 long ladder		8	0
2 ladders		7	0
2 sheep racks		2	0
4 cow crips		3	6
1 grind stone & frame		4	0
1 goose coop & hen coop		2	6
2 pig troughs		1	9

The list continues with sections for the horses, pigs, dairy, cellar, kitchen, large and small parlours, chambers over parlour and dairy, attic, storm room, brewhouse, and garden.

ACCOUNT BOOKS

Account books record financial dealings. Here is an extract from John Dent's account book from High Green Farm, Mickleton, Co. Durham:

1765 some of his outgoings			
Lord's rent	£3	4s	$4\frac{1}{2}$d
Land tax	£2	10s	4d
Window tax		14s	
Poor tax		16s	
His 1792 tythe to the rector			
2 lambs at 3s 6d		7s	0d
5 fleeces at 1s		5s	0d
1 swarm of bees			1d
1 foal		1s	0d
$\frac{1}{2}$ a calf		13s	

THE BOARD OF AGRICULTURE, 1793–1822

This was an information service run by the government. It made reports on farming in each county. Find out what the Board wrote about your county. A copy may be in your record office or library.

ACTS OF PARLIAMENT FOR ENCLOSURE

See pages 36–42 where an example of enclosure is dealt with in full. Enclosure Acts resulted in major changes in the layout of the farms and village life.

OTHER SOURCES

These include pictures painted or drawn at the time, farming textbooks, leaflets about farming, farmstead plans, machinery catalogues and Ministry of Agriculture publications. There are several examples of such sources in this book. On the next page is an information sheet issued by Whitfield Example Farm in Gloucestershire in 1844, which published the results of its experiments.

WHITFIELD EXAMPLE FARM.

The course of cropping adopted on this farm, is that which takes off the same ground, alternately, a crop of roots or green food for stock, and a seed producing crop as food for man.

The following table shews the manner in which the farm was cropped last year, the way in which it is cropped this year, and the mode of cropping which it is proposed to adopt in 1843 and 4; and as the course of cropping is uniform over the whole farm, the crop for any future year on the several fields may be easily ascertained by an examination of the table.

From this table it will be seen that clovers or seeds are taken once in six years; swedes, turnips, or cole once in six years; carrots once in twelve years; mangel-wurzel and potatoes once in 24 years; wheat once in four years; and corn, which may be oats, barley, beans, pease, vetches, or wheat once in four years.

The whole of the clover or seed is consumed on the land by sheep, and all the root crop, (80 acres) dunged every year with farm yard dung, made in the yards or folds of the farm.

No of Field.	Crops, 1841.	Crops, 1842.	Crops, 1843.	Crops, 1844.
1	Mangel-wurzel.	Wheat & Beans	Swedes.	Corn, (wheat?)
2	Oats	Carrots,	Wheat.	Swedes.
3	Swedes.	Beans & Potatoes.	Carrots.	Wheat.
4	Wheat.	Clover.	Corn, (wheat?)	Carrots.
5	Swedes & Turnips.	Wheat.	Clover.	Corn, (wheat?)
6	Beans & Oats.	Swedes.	Wheat.	Clover.
7	Swedes.	Wheat.	Turnips.	Wheat.
8	Oats.	Mangel-wurzel.	Corn, (wheat?)	Turnips.
9	Clover.	Wheat.	Mangel-wurzel.	Corn, (wheat?)
10	Wheat.	Clover.	Wheat.	Mangel-wurzel.
11	Carrots & Potatoes.	Wheat & Beans.	Clover.	Wheat.
12	Wheat.	Swedes.	Corn, (wheat?)	Clover.
13	Clover.	Wheat.	Swedes.	Corn, (wheat?)
14	Wheat.	Carrots & Swedes.	Wheat.	Swedes.
15	Swedes.	Wheat.	Carrots.	Wheat.
16	Oats.	Clover.	Corn, (oats.)	Carrots.
17	Wheat.	Clover.	Clover.	Corn, (oats.)
18	Wheat & Oats.	Turnips & Cole.	Wheat.	Clover.
19	Clover.	Oats.	Cole.	Wheat.
20	Wheat.	Clover.	Corn, (oats.)	Cole.
21	Oats.	Turnips.	Potatoes.	Corn, (oats.)
22	Oats.	Turnips.	Wheat.	Potatoes.
23	Old Grass.	Oats.	Clover.	Wheat.
24	Old Grass.	Oats.	Beans.	Clover.

Whitfield Example Farm information sheet, 1844. A detailed booklet on horse-handling and ploughing was also issued.

FURTHER READING

Beresford, M. *History on the Ground* (Lutterworth Press, 1957)
Harley, J. B. *Maps for the Local Historian* (Bedford Square Press, 1972)

4 Evidence on the Ground

(a)   Landscape History

Unfortunately remains are not easy to detect today, as they are difficult to tell apart from natural features. You can start by examining a large-scale map, which may mark medieval villages or field systems. But it will not show everything, and so you will get a chance really to *discover* things on the ground for yourself.

AERIAL PHOTOGRAPHY

A good way to begin is by using aerial photographs. Because earthworks may be very large, it is often not easy to spot their shapes. Aerial photographs may reveal patterns of old fields, even medieval strip patterns, which are not visible from the ground.

If you are lucky, your record office or library may have an aerial photograph of the site you are working on. If not, one way to take aerial photographs is to use a *delta kite*. Hang the camera on a cradle 30 m below the kite and fly it at a height of about 100 m. Control the shutter release by radio control. A windspeed of 10–20 m.p.h. is best.

An easier, but more expensive, way is to use a remote control *model aircraft*. You will have better control of the camera and so get better pictures. It is best to take photographs in low sunlight so as to increase the shadows, and you should aim to take your shots at an angle rather than straight down. Remains often show up as soil marks or disturbances made by man and will be revealed in texture and colour on the photograph. Make sure you get permission from the farmer first, and take care not to disturb animals. Watch out for electricity cables. (See page 34.)

FIELD ARCHAEOLOGY

You will probably not be allowed to excavate what you detect by aerial photography, but you can carry out *field archaeology*. That means patiently studying the site. Look for important clues to how land has been used, such as soil type, vegetation and the lie of the land. What seems an exciting discovery from an aerial photograph may be nothing more than a spot where a dead animal was recently buried! Nettles suggest recent human disturbance; so do common arable weeds. From the air a place where old houses once stood may look the same as a shallow gravel pit. Only a close look will tell – a house site is likely to be more rectangular.

Aerial photograph of Byfield Hill, near Woodford Halse, Northants

It is important to measure earthworks carefully, as sizes may provide clues about the age and type of the remains. On arable land it is best to investigate when the ground is either bare or just sown. On grass and moorland the best times are in winter and spring, before new growth has occurred. For woodland, winter is best.

EARLY BUILDINGS AND VILLAGES

Very few of the buildings we see today were built before 1500. Even those that survive are not typical, as they were usually houses for richer people and often have been altered a good deal. Little remains of ordinary villagers' houses, but information about them can be obtained from archaeological excavations, surface remains and archives.

Buildings built before 1500 were often made of wood, turf or baked earth, which has long since rotted away. They were also not well-built, and probably only lasted about 30 years before they needed rebuilding. So, when digging on a site, it is often difficult to know the exact shape of a house, as it may have been rebuilt several times.

In Chysauster, Cornwall, eight stone houses have been discovered, built in two rows in the second century B.C. They were probably lived in for around 400 years. Each had a courtyard and a round room where pottery was found.

DESERTED MEDIEVAL VILLAGES

These can be seen as mounds on the ground. In some places villages have become smaller rather than dis-appearing altogether. So far over 2000 deserted medieval villages have been found – some by schoolchildren. (See the case study on pages 33–5.)

How do we know whether a mound is a house site or not? It is difficult to be certain at ground level, because of the earth and grass covering the site. So be very careful. An aerial photograph might help – a group of mounds alongside what appears to be a road could well represent old houses. So could many mounds laid out around a village green, or near a church.

There is no single size for a typical medieval house to help us. *Longhouses* (see page 16) occur in some parts of the country. They are usually 15 m in length, but poorer peasants might have had only a small, one-roomed building of 5 m. In the claylands of the Midlands, houses were often built on a platform surrounded by a ditch. In well-drained areas houses may have been surrounded by walls, hedges or fenced banks. What traces would these leave?

A moated site near Woburn. What can you deduce from this photograph?

10

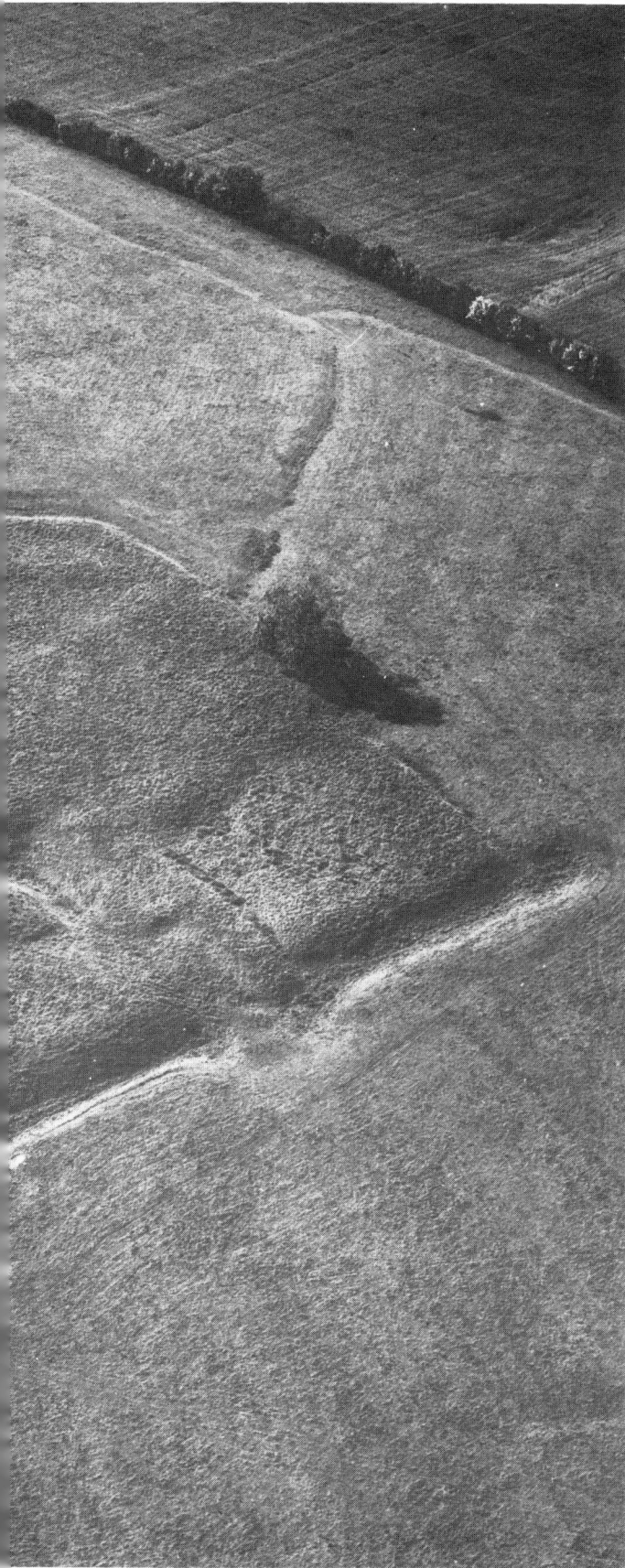

MOATED SITES

Five thousand of these sites have been traced from aerial photographs and from study on the ground. Moated sites are usually dry or perhaps marshy today, rather than still full of water. They tend to be square or rectangular, though a few are round. The moats are often U-shaped or with a flat bottom. In the middle there is a platform. These sites can be found almost anywhere – near or in existing villages, or on their own. Several may be close together or inside one another. Their size depends on what was built on the central platform. It might have been a manor house or several buildings. Smaller sites may have had chapels or windmills. They tend to be pre-1500, and are usually found on clay soils.

It is difficult to tell what they were used for. Most are too small for defence purposes. Was it to protect the wooden buildings inside from fire? Or perhaps to keep animals out, or simply to supply fresh water or store fish? Shallow hollows, however, may well be fishponds if they are quite regular in shape and flat-bottomed. Remember that hollows cutting *through* medieval ridges and furrows must be later than them in date.

FIELDS

Do not think that the large fields of today were always there. Fields change too. Ploughing of fields goes back a long way. Scratch marks have been found in Wiltshire, possibly made by a plough 5000 years ago. Prehistoric fields are still fairly common in Dorset and Yorkshire. Surrounded by earth banks formed by ploughing, these so-called *Celtic fields* are square or rectangular in shape, and about half a hectare in area. Most surviving prehistoric fields may be found on hillsides. Roman fields survive only in some parts. They were often similar to prehistoric ones, though slightly larger.

RIDGE AND FURROW

This is the name given to strip farming begun in the Saxon period. It is produced by regular ploughing up and down the same furrows year after year. The soil thrown up gradually creates the mounds of the ridges, especially in the Midland heavy clay areas. Take care, though, for later ploughing can produce a similar effect and so can the laying of underground drainage. Even animals and frost can produce similar effects.

To make sure it is a ridge and furrow system, mark out the shape of the furrows with poles, or even with people standing at regular intervals. Medieval furrows often resemble a backward S-shape. This was probably due to

11

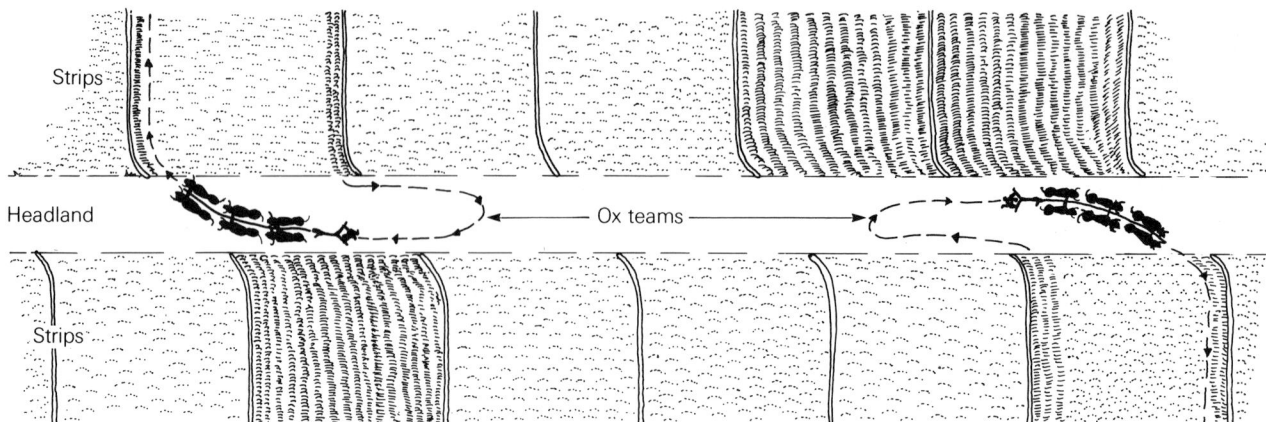

Oxen ploughing on the S-turn system

the oxen saving turning space by veering off to the left at the end of a strip. Look at the hedges nearby, as S-shaped ones may provide a clue. Such hedges date from before 1400, as this method of ploughing seems to have ended about then.

Check, too, whether anything has later been built over the top of the ridge and furrow. If a canal has been cut through it, the system must date from before the canal. If it continues on the other side of a well-established hedge, then it must be older than the hedge. Also, older furrows were probably deeper than later ones, and old ridges tended to be slightly wider.

TERRACING

Terracing, called *lynchets*, on hill-sides is a feature to look for, especially in Dorset and Yorkshire. Lynchets vary in height and width, but many are medieval. They were probably created to provide extra ground for crops.

LAND ENCLOSURE

The farm land you will find today was mainly the result of enclosing the open fields and common land of a medieval village. In medieval times the village usually had three large fields divided into $\frac{1}{2}$ acre (0.2 hectare) strips, separated by ridges of earth. Each farmer had a number of strips in each field and had to grow the same crops as everyone else did. So the farmers lived in the village itself as it was central to all the fields. The common land was available to all for such purposes as grazing animals and collecting wood.

Enclosures for sheep farming occurred in the fifteenth and sixteenth centuries, and then in the eighteenth and early nineteenth centuries whole villages abandoned their open fields for personal enclosed farms (see pages 36–42). It was then possible for farmers to build *Hanoverian* farmsteads in the centre of their new farms (see page 20). Fields which are long, thin and curved,

Strip lynchets in Dorset

Middle Ditchford, a Gloucestershire hamlet. Spot the medieval streets, house mounds, and ridges and furrows made by ploughing. The village was deserted when sheep farming was developed there in the fifteenth century.

with curving roads round them, will probably have been enclosed early on. Those which are small and squarish with straight roads are likely to be later enclosures.

HEDGE-BANK DATING

Some historians say hedges in lowland England – that is, excluding the highland zones of the north and west where the soil is acidic – can be dated by counting the number of species in a 30 m section. Even allowing for soil, climate and varying degrees of care, each different species indicates about 100 years of a hedge's life. Thus a one-species hedge is about 100 years old, and a five-species one 500 years old. You must ignore herbs, brambles and nettles. You can use one of two formulas worked out by historians for dating a hedge. Either (a)

age of hedge $= (99 \times$ number of species$) - 16$; or (b) age of hedge $= (110 \times$ number of species$) + 30$. The fact that these formulas are different shows historians disagree about how to make such assessments.

Other historians claim these formulas are unreliable, as it is only too easy to confuse different leaves, or disagree on whether species should be sub-divided or not. They say more accurate dating can be obtained by examining old maps. If the hedges are curved or in the form of a reverse 'S' they are enclosed field strips, while small irregular fields predate the Black Death, and fields with straight edges are ones enclosed between 1750 and 1850. Names such as Orchard Close and Kitchen Fields are early as they refer to fields used by manor houses. All one can claim from counting, they argue, is that fields with four or less shrubs are 1750–1850, while those with more are likely to be older.

13

ROADS AND PATHWAYS

All roads were man-made, and so must have had a purpose. Prehistoric *causeways* were to cross fenland or bogs. Prehistoric man used *ridgeways* along the uplands too. The Romans built about 10 000 miles of straight *main* roads which can be spotted on maps quite easily. They also built many minor roads, some of which are still to be discovered.

Look for a length of Roman road near you on an O.S. map. It may appear to 'run out', but when you get on site you may be able to find the rest of it. Roman roads were often built on an *agger*, a raised mound that allowed for drainage. Thus the mound may remain even if the road does not. Later farming may have ploughed or hedged over the Roman roads, so that the modern road suddenly turns sharply; the Roman road would have carried on in a straight line.

Very deep roads, with high banks and thick hedges, may belong to the period soon after the Romans left. They probably mark the boundaries of land areas laid out in Saxon times. But they may be older. Check the date of the hedges to see.

The routes used for taking animals to market are called *drover roads*, and they may be 900 years old. The depth of these roads will show if they have been used for a long time. Look out for 'Drover's Arms' pub signs. Look out for old paths, perhaps between house plots or to deserted medieval village sites, on aerial photographs. Documentary evidence may help. (See Chapter 3.)

Paved Roman road over Blackstone Edge, Yorkshire

FURTHER READING

M. Cottrell, The Kite Store, 69 Neal Street, London, WC2H 9PJ, can supply kites for aerial photography. His booklet, *Low Altitude Aerial Photography from Kites and Balloons* (1983), gives full details and advice.

Other books:
Bagshawe, R. W. *Roman Roads* (Shire Publications, 1979)
Garner, L. *Dry-Stone Walls* (Shire Publications, 1984)
Harvey, N. *Fields, Hedges and Ditches* (Shire Publications, 1976)
Harvey, N. *Trees, Woods and Forests* (Shire Publications, 1981)
Hindle, B. P. *Medieval Roads* (Shire Publications, 1982)
Hooper, M. D. *Hedges and Local History* (Bedford Square Press, 1971)
Muir, R. and N. *Hedgerows, Their History and Wildlife* (Michael Joseph, 1987)
Riley, D. N. *Aerial Archaeology in Britain* (Shire Publications, 1982)
Roberts, B. K. *Village Plans* (Shire Publications, 1982)
Rowley, T. and Wood, J. *Deserted Villages* (Shire Publications, 1982)
Wilson, D. *Moated Sites* (Shire Publications, 1982)

(b) Farmsteads

BASIC POINTS TO NOTE

WHAT IS A FARMSTEAD?

It is the operations centre of a business. In come animals, seed, fodder and machines; out go manure, grain, milk, butter, cheese and animals. The farmstead consists of a farmhouse and the buildings and yards needed to run the business.

THE SITE OF A FARMSTEAD

Why was it built there? Why were the buildings grouped in a particular way, and facing the direction they are?

The siting will have been determined by:

(a) *Soil* To get fertile, well-drained arable land *and* poorer soil for rough pasture, it is best to choose the point where two different types of soil meet. Ideal soil is light and *porous* (able to soak up water) on top of *impermeable* ('waterproof') clay or rock. In such conditions water soaks into the soil, but does not go deeper than the crop's roots.

(b) *Shelter* This may be vital in the wet, windy west of the UK.

(c) *Water supply* Streams, springs, etc. are essential.

(d) *Need for a central position* In the days of 'strip' farming in large open fields, the nearest a person could get to all his strips was to be in the centre of the two- or three-field system. So cottages were grouped together in the centre of their farming area. When the land was reorganised to produce compact 'enclosed' farms, the farmer would have wanted his buildings in the centre of his own farm.

Farmsteads may be closely grouped together, which means they date back to the time of strip farming. They may be in groups of two or three, which suggest the remains of a village. Isolated farms mean either that the area has been occupied by a single farm ever since it was first farmed (at any time since the Norman Conquest), or that the farmstead was built when the village's land was enclosed.

EXAMINING FARMSTEADS

Remember, there will have been huge changes over the centuries on any farm. Some buildings were built for a definite purpose, while others had to be adapted to a new function as times changed. Try to work out the original purposes of the buildings you see, as well as their present uses. You can spot whether a building has been altered by looking for the use of later materials, the moving of a doorway or window, the redesigning of the interior, etc.

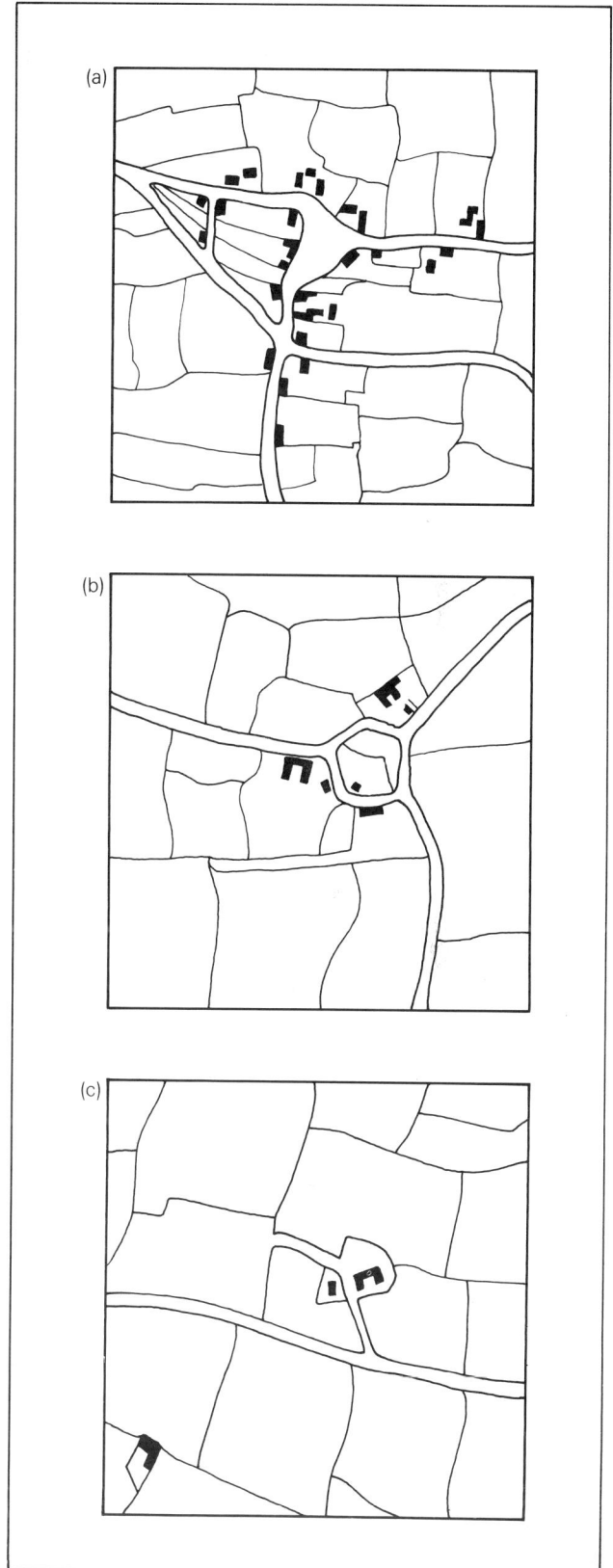

Farmsteads in (a) a village, (b) a small group, (c) isolated with field barn arrangement

First, you need to know something of the history and layout of farm buildings and their uses. Two basic layouts are the longhouse and the courtyard farm.

1. LONGHOUSES

These are generally easy to identify, as their name suggests. They were designed to house the animals at one end and the farmer and his family at the other end, with space for storage too. Look for signs of the original divisions. Later longhouses were divided by walls into three sections, for the family, livestock and storage. Longhouses were for small-scale peasant farmers of the Middle Ages, who looked after 20–30 acres. They built them in upland areas such as Wales, the Lake District and Dartmoor. Their building was forbidden in the 1920s as unhygienic.

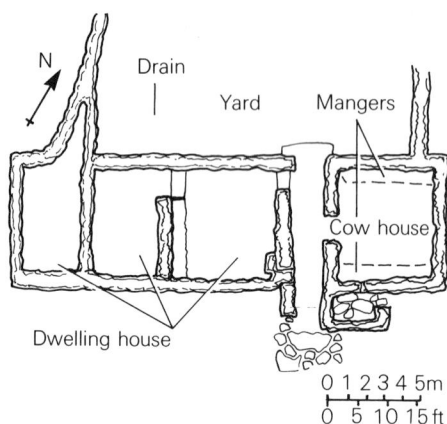

A plan of a longhouse

2. COURTYARD FARMS

These were designed to provide good protection from the weather and marauders. Besides the farmhouse a courtyard farm has three parts: the yard, barns and livestock buildings.

It is possible that the farm you visit may be a really old one, a *manor farmstead*. Wealthier farmers of the Middle Ages would group their buildings round a *yard*. The main building was the *barn* – perhaps two, one for the corn to be used on the farm and one for storing the rest before sale. The barn would be on the north side to give protection to the south-facing yard. Livestock houses and yards were placed so as to benefit from the shelter the barn could provide. The farming process began in the stack yard on the far side of the barn; into this came corn sheaves, and out of the barn came the grain to make bread and the straw for the animals. Out of the livestock houses came straw turned into manure, to help grow more crops.

In good quarry areas – within a 75 mile radius of Bristol, for example – whole buildings of manor farmsteads were made of stone. Elsewhere the bottom sections were made of stone, and the rest was made with timber and *wattle and daub* (interwoven twigs with mud or clay plastered over them). *Cruck* structures involved frameworks of roughly squared timbers, split into two and set opposite each other either in the earth or on a stone base. The crucks formed arches, and the rest of the framework and building could be constructed round them.

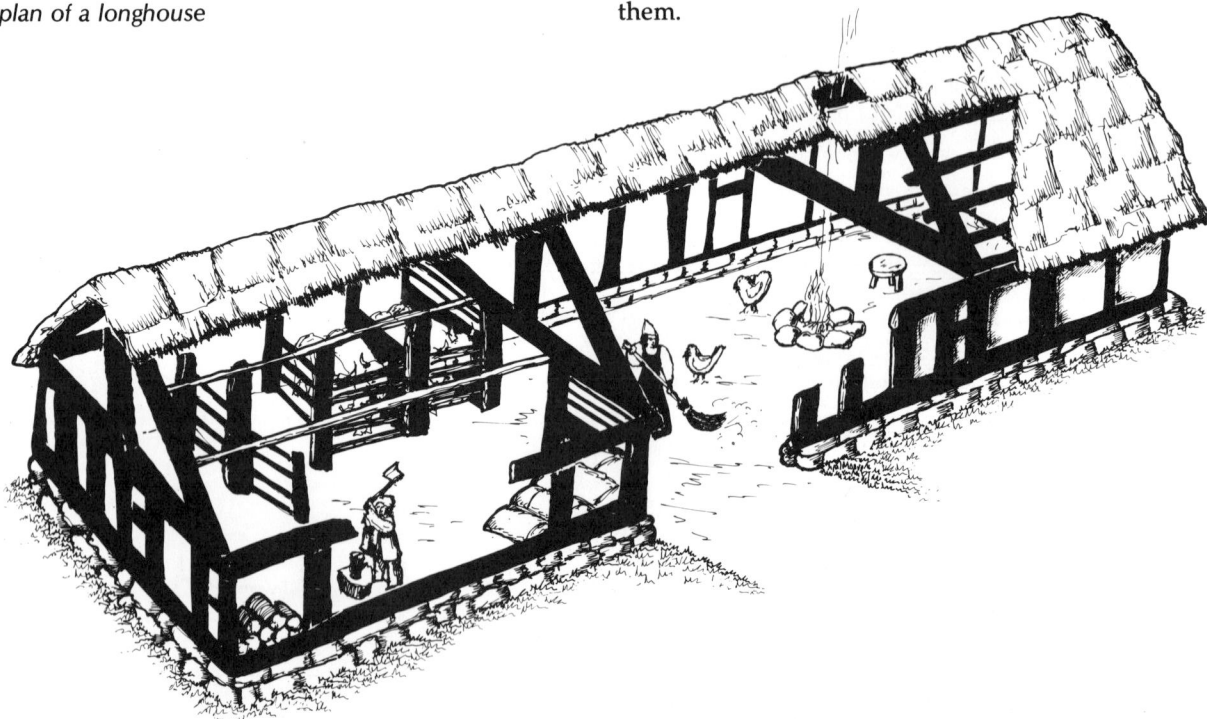

Reconstruction of longhouse at Wharram Percy, N. Yorkshire. This is a pre-Norman house, with stone foundations, timber frames, wattle and daub panels and a straw roof. Oxen and sheep would have been penned, chickens loose. There is a central hearth with a smoke hole in the roof.

A cruck barn in Herefordshire

A Nottinghamshire Hanoverian farm of the early nineteenth century. Identify the various buildings.

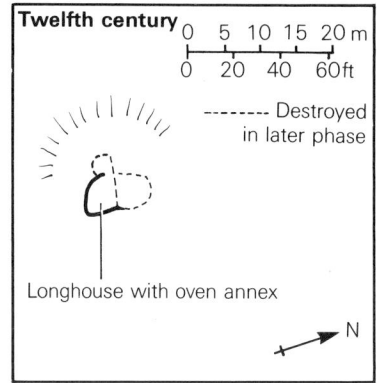

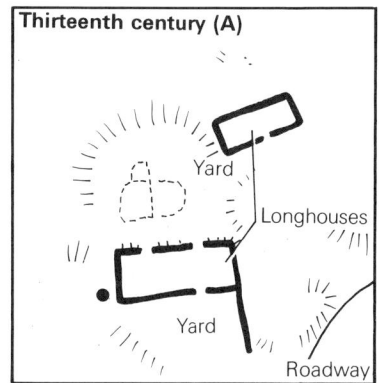

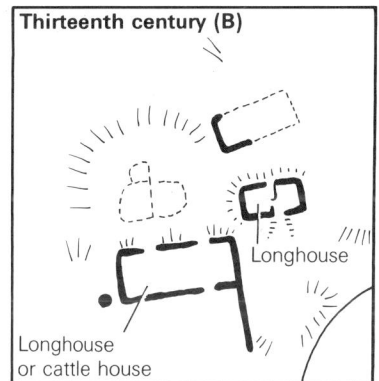

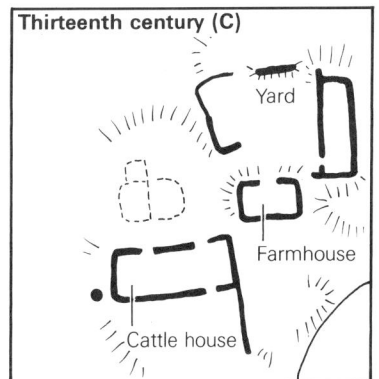

Twelfth century

0 5 10 15 20 m
0 20 40 60ft

------ Destroyed in later phase

Longhouse with oven annex

N

Thirteenth century (A)

Yard

Longhouses

Yard

Roadway

Thirteenth century (B)

Longhouse

Longhouse or cattle house

Thirteenth century (C)

Yard

Farmhouse

Cattle house

The development of a medieval farmstead in Wiltshire from basic longhouse to early courtyard farm

Look at the series of pictures of farm buildings below and opposite. There were originally two separate buildings, a farmhouse and a barn. Then in the 1740s the farmer added a building to link those two, and then a brick one on the end. Notice how you can work out the relative ages of the buildings by looking at the materials they were made from. Clues to follow are the timber frames, the uneven stone work, the sizes and shapes of the windows, the thickness of the walls and the shapes and sizes of the bricks.

Now look at the plan and measured drawing of one of the barns. There is a bricked-up opening and a door set 2 m from the ground. The plan suggests that this was the old threshing barn which you can see in the photograph. The opening was for the driving shaft of the threshing machine. This machine was powered by two horses which walked round and round in the gin gang shed, or wheelhouse. The photograph of the Devon farm on page 23 shows the horses' work shed clearly, as well as a waterwheel which was added later. Then the horses were no longer used. The doorway was above ground level because it was originally reached by a ramp. The straw left over from the threshing was then tossed out of the doorway at the end of the barn into the yard below.

Look again at the photographs of the buildings. What materials have been used? If you are studying a farm you will need to photograph or sketch such features and measure them up, so as to work out their original uses. Have those uses changed in any way?

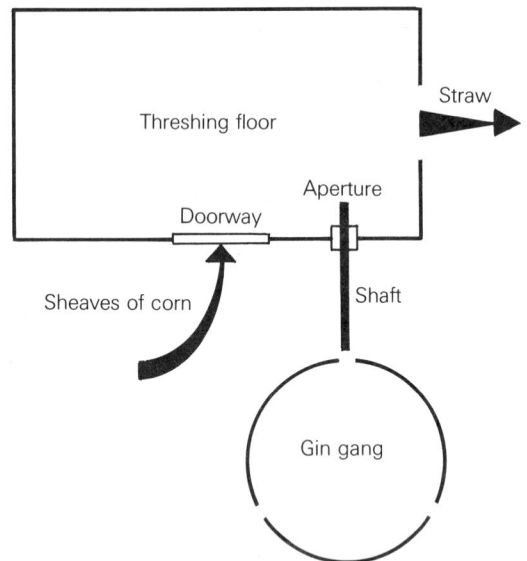

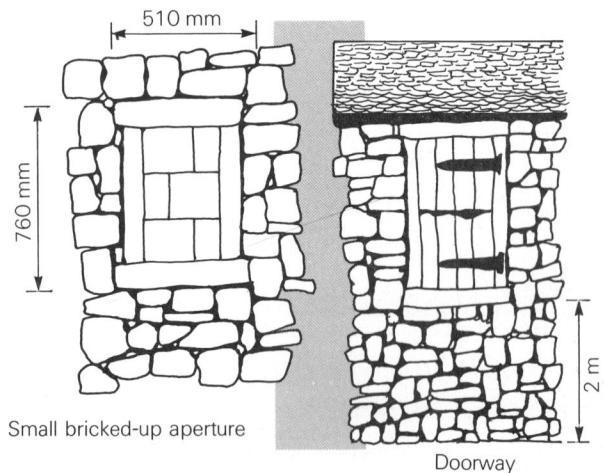

Developments in the buildings of a Northumberland farm

The old threshing barn

Cowsheds

The old threshing barn

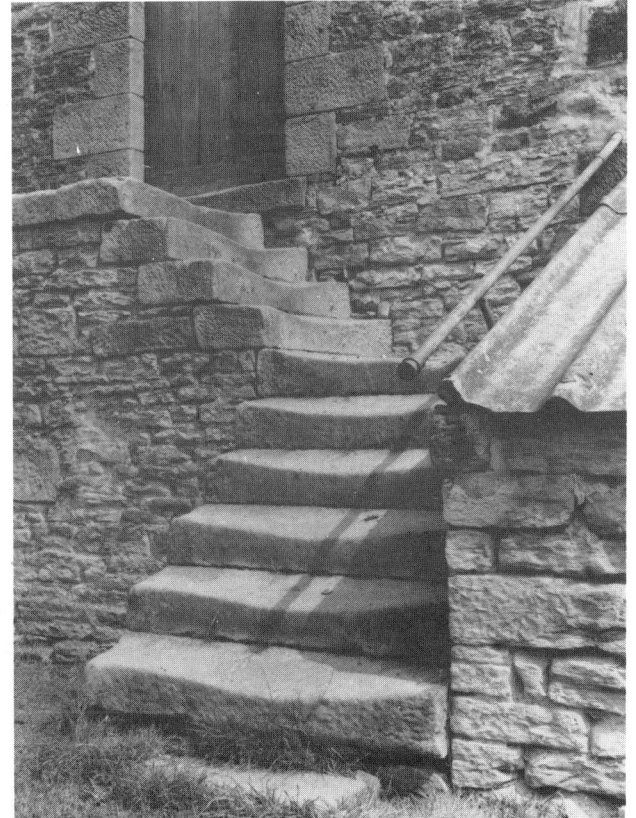

Steps up to the granary

When you visit a farm, see if you can work out the eighteenth-century plan behind its layout. The layout was chiefly aimed to make daily chores convenient to do, just as people today plan the layout of a new kitchen to make things easy to reach. Some points to think about: What daily farmyard chores would benefit from a careful layout of buildings? Why might a farmstead be thought of as a 'muck factory'? In what ways is the yard all important? Why would straw be put in the yard? Remember the cattle would spend the winter in the yard. What would be the effect of cattle trampling on straw and manure?

The new enclosed farms of the eighteenth century encouraged landowners to build their Hanoverian or Georgian farmsteads in the middle of their land, rather than forcing their tenant farmers to walk every day from the centre of the village. Instead of a farmer just adding an extra building to his collection, he could, for the first time in centuries, plan a complete set of buildings. D. Garrett produced his *Designs and Estimates of Farmhouses* in 1747 to suggest ways of doing this.

On-site farmsteads would be more efficient. The staff would not have to move the animals so far, and the distance for taking crops to barns and manure to fields would be cut down. The farmer could keep a close eye on his animals, staff and property if he lived on site, and especially if his farmhouse was placed so that he could watch what went on in his yards and sheds. When you visit a farm, see if the farmhouse gives the farmer a commanding view or not. (Also see if you can find an office there. If so, it will show that the farm is becoming more like a factory than a household.)

A farmstead of about 1800. What type of farm is it? How could you date it by looking at the picture? What seem to be the jobs of (a) women, (b) men, (c) children? What materials have been used to build the farmstead?

20

PARTS OF THE FARMSTEAD

This next section looks at parts of the farmstead in more detail.

1. THE YARD

The yard is the centrepiece of the farmstead. Here the livestock are exercised and the manure collected. It usually faces south to get the sun and avoid the south-westerly rain and winds. What shelters it on the north side? Take a compass to check whether this is so on the farm you visit.

You may come across the term *bedded yard*. This refers to a yard in which livestock lie down on bedding, in which the dung is mixed as it falls. It is covered at intervals with a fresh bedding of straw. Over a full winter, cattle yards can create a bed of up to 1.5 m depth. The manure is used as fertiliser.

The effects of the depression years of 1870–1900, the 1920s and the 1930s can often be seen if you look carefully round a yard. Notice where second-hand materials have been used: railway sleepers from the 1890s onwards (for walls of sheds and yards), old railway wagons in the 1920s, and Nissen huts after World War I. Barns ceased to be repaired and came to be used for any kind of storage. Concrete was used more, especially for the floors of cowhouses and dung channels. Corrugated-iron sheeting came in, and in the 1930s was superseded by asbestos-cement sheeting, which gave better insulation and did not need maintenance.

2. BARNS

The feature of barns most likely to catch your eye is the pair of large doors in the centre for wagons to enter. Check the positions of doors in the barns you examine. Two on opposite sides of the barn were not only needed to create the draught for *winnowing* (see below); but they were also essential for ox-carts, as oxen cannot go backwards! The taller door on one side was for the laden carts to enter by, while the lower one opposite was for the empty ones to leave by. Notice the porches, which not only gave protection to the interior but also provided parking space for the wagons, keeping them away from the threshing floor. Examine the doors to see if they have space for *spurting boards* (see below).

Pay particular attention to the barn floor. It had to be hard so that in winter the labourers could thresh the corn. The threshing floor was made of oak boards or hard stone or a mixture of clay, sand, water, chalk, chaff, cow-dung and bullocks' blood, put down in 1 in. (2.5 cm) layers to a thickness of about 4 in. (10 cm).

Is there a loft in the barn? If so, it was installed when that farm started using a threshing machine sometime after 1786. It was needed to feed the corn into the top of the machine, which stood on the threshing floor. Is there a *pitching hole* high up in the wall, for off-loading cart loads into the barn to await threshing? Look for air vents, and for square or circular holes about 15–20 cm across to allow owls in to catch vermin.

Threshing by hand involved farm labourers beating at it with flails. Two men would tackle a dozen sheaves at a time, beating them at the rate of about 30 strokes a minute. They would rake the straw off when the loose corn was a foot (30 cm) high. The task went on for months. Then they winnowed *it, tossing it so that the unwanted chaff could blow away. The two doors opposite to each other in the barn provided the draught for winnowing. Often the doors did not reach the ground, the gap being filled by a plank, called a* spurting board, *resting on notches. This was to stop grain escaping when it was flailed, while still allowing for a draught during winnowing. They could process up to 12 bushels (about 440 litres) of wheat a day. The threshed corn was then stacked at either end of the barn.*

Threshing by flail. Is the spurting board in use?

21

If you live in Staffordshire, Suffolk or Sussex, look for eighteenth-century *cornholes*. These were put in to house the mixed grain and chaff after threshing until enough was ready for winnowing.

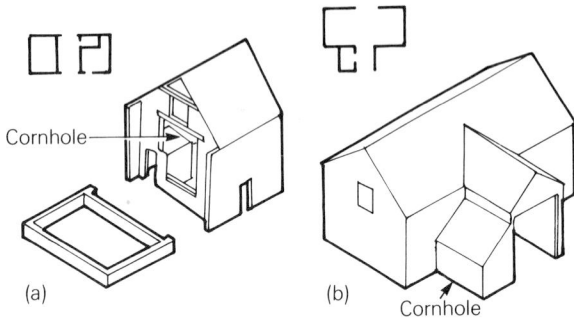

Cornholes (a) in Staffordshire (about 1 m wide and 2 m high) and (b) in Suffolk.

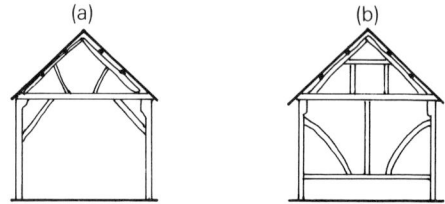

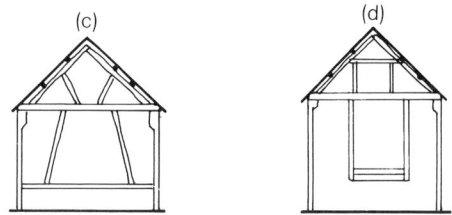

Tithe barns

The term *tithe barn* should really refer only to barns where the village tithe-holder (see page 3) stored his property; but it is often used to mean any medieval barn. Tithe barns were huge stone and timber structures with church-like interiors. If you find one with narrow doors it is medieval, as the tithes were brought in by hand or in the horse-panniers (baskets carried by horses). Later tithe barns had cart-sized doors. If there is an internal division in the barn, it will have been added in the seventeenth century or later, to separate the storage bays from the threshing floors. Look for the braces strengthening the walls against the wind outside and the pressure of the stacked grain inside. *Aisled* barns (with extra bays) enabled barns as wide as 15 m to be built, which meant they did not have to be so long.

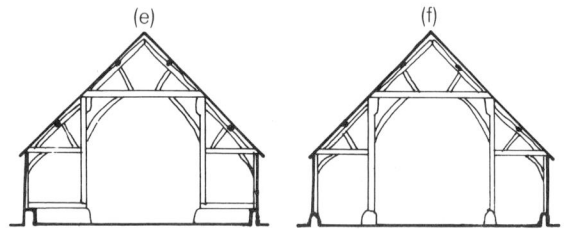

Internal divisions in barns: (a) open; (b) timber-framed; (c) later timber-framed; (d) brick spur walls; (e) aisled with tie between foot of main posts and outer wall; (f) aisled without tie

Tisbury tithe barn, Shaftesbury, the largest tithe barn in England. It is 60 m long and 270 tonnes of reeds were needed to thatch its 120 m roof to a depth of 300 mm in 1971. It took five men four months to thatch it and their work will last 70 years.

This Devon farm has a Hanoverian wheelhouse and a Victorian waterwheel which replaced the horse power.

Wheelhouses (gin gangs)

Following Andrew Meikle's invention of the mechanical threshing machine in 1786, wheelhouses attached to barns became a feature. Horses powered the machines by walking round and round. A four-horse wheel did 3 r.p.m. at $2\frac{1}{4}$ m.p.h., turning an 8 m diameter wheel set 2.5 m off the ground. This meant that the largest wheelhouses were 9 m by 4.5 m. A two-horse wheel could thresh 120 bushels (4400 litres) of oats or 60 bushels (2200 litres) of wheat in 8 hours. Is there a wheelhouse in your area? If so, what machinery still remains?

Steam power came next. If a tall chimney is attached to the barn you can be sure that steam power was used. The introduction of traction engines meant threshing could be done in the fields rather than in barns.

A granary, built in 1731, from Littlehampton, now in the Weald and Downland Museum near Chichester. Its 6 m^2 stands on sixteen staddles, which is unusual. Most stand on nine staddles about 2 m apart, with the sides of the granary measuring about 4 m.

Granaries

Granaries (grain stores) mounted on supports called *staddles*, to keep out rats and mice, were built in the seventeenth and eighteenth centuries. Check to see if the floor planks were fitted as tightly as possible. Why would this have been done?

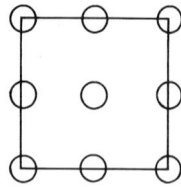

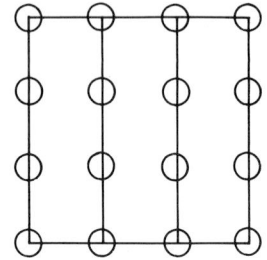

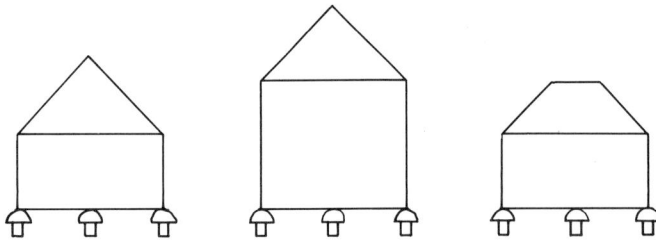

The most usual forms in the South East on 9 staddles

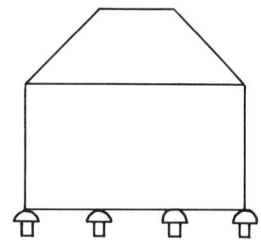

The Littlehampton granary

The usual forms of staddles in South East England, as compared with the Littlehampton granary

Rick yards

See if the farm you visit has the remains of a stone platform, with anti-rat 'flared' or overlapping stones on top. (Alternatively there may be an iron platform made by Thomas Pearson & Co.) If so, it is the remains of a rick yard. They were in use in the early nineteenth century to provide additional storage space. It was a cheaper and better way of storage than traditional barns. You should find such rick yards on the north side of a farm, screened off by elm trees. They had a slight slope leading to a drainage ditch. Corrugated iron roofs were useful against the new hazard of sparks from steam trains. Rick burning was a frequent form of vandalism, too.

Stone platform for a rick

A tall tower silo at Braby Knee, Trowbridge

Silos

Silos made of concrete, steel or brick are a feature you are likely to see. They were designed to solve the problem of winter feed for the livestock. Hay could not be relied upon, and root crops were too expensive. Silage-making was a crude way of 'canning' grass. If stored undried in an airtight pit or container it was not affected by the weather. In the late 1880s, 2600 silos were in use. Some were lined pits; others were adapted barns. In 1901 Wye College farm tried a wooden tower type. You may find the old-style *clamps* (that is, walls holding the feed) often made of old railway sleepers or concrete slabs.

Tall tower silos are American-style ones dating from the late 1950s. They were airtight, glass-lined steel con-tainers which kept the oxygen out. They looked impressive, compared to the clamps with their walls, railway sleepers or concrete slabs (although cattle were able to feed themselves from the clamps).

Dutch barns

You may find large prefabricated steel barns with light curved roofs of corrugated iron. They were built from the 1880s, on the design of eighteenth-century Dutch timber barns. They were cheap and adaptable as they were simply skeleton buildings. Hay or straw was originally stored in them. How does the farmer use them today?

25

Dutch barns in Yorkshire

3. LIVESTOCK BUILDINGS

Try to distinguish those built for work animals from those for cattle. You should find livestock buildings set at right angles to the barn, arranged in the order in which straw from the barn was most needed. Hence the cattle-fattening shed was nearest; next the young cattle shed; then the cowshed, and finally the sheds for oxen and horses. The latter faced east to greet the morning sun. Why would oxen and horses need the morning sun? You will find the pigsty was nearest to the farmhouse. Why would the farmer or his wife find that position useful? The poultry would be kept nearby, too. Why?

The animals in the livestock buildings could process their manure by trampling it into the straw and hay put on the floor.

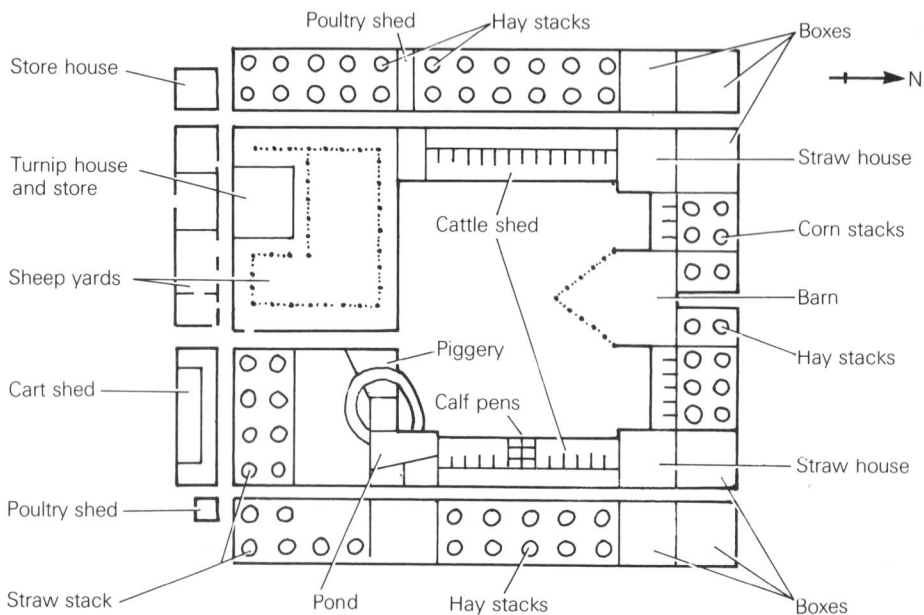

A drawing of a possible model farm published in 1770. Why are the buildings arranged in the order they are around the yard? What good and bad points about the design can you spot?

26

Dairies and cowhouses

In the 1880s there were 2 million dairy cows in England and Wales; by the 1930s, 3 million. Laws were now affecting milk production. The Dairies, Cowsheds and Milkshops Order, 1885, gave local authorities power to make by-laws (local laws) on the design and construction of dairy buildings. Dairies had originally been built at the back of farmhouses, but in the nineteenth century, to ensure no contamination from farmyard waste, they were placed elsewhere.

See if there is sufficient ventilation, window lighting and air space for each cow. Concrete floors with dung channels and drains were a big improvement. The idea of a permanent *milking parlour* on the farmstead was first tried by A. J. Hosier in Wiltshire in 1932. It was a building planned round a machine, without stalls for cows to live in.

Different designs of dairy buildings have been used over the years. The *loose housing* design has a yard for the cows to live in as well as a milking section. In the yard, they tread their manure through its slatted floor into a cellar, from which it can be collected. The *cubicle housing* design allows each cow a stall with access to its food.

The 'model' mid-Victorian cowhouse illustrated below was more hygienic than most cowhouses of its time. How has cast iron been used in this building? What is the trolley for? How is the fodder arrangement made?

A 'model' Victorian cowhouse

Diagram labels (top — mid-Victorian cowhouse)

Overhead loft for hay and straw – a source of dust

2 m

Rough brick walls – difficult to clean

Earth or chalk floor

3.75 m

Diagram labels (bottom — 1930s cowhouse)

Ventilating outlet

Roof lights

Concrete partition

Impervious insulated concrete floor

Concrete manger with glazed surface

2.5 m

Dung channel for effective drainage

4.5 m

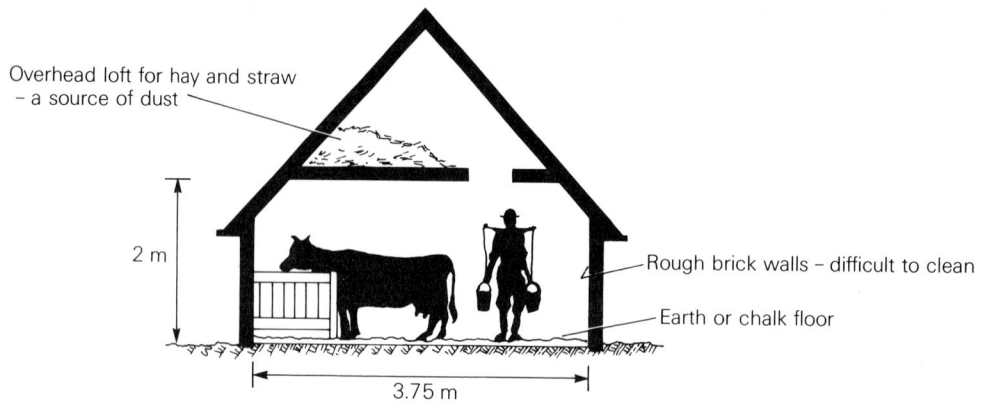

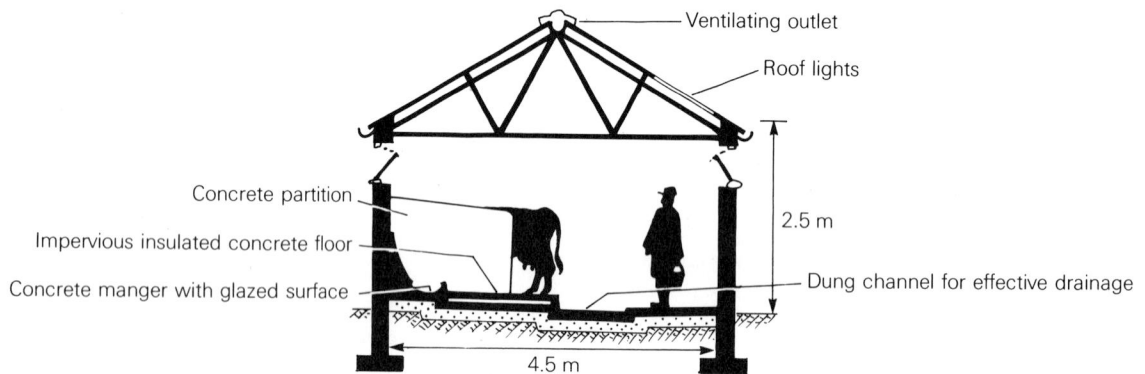

Compare the mid-Victorian cowhouse (top) with that of the 1930s (bottom). How has concrete been used? How and why has the roof been changed?

Pigs

A variety of housing methods have been used. *Pen-and-run piggeries* (for sleeping and exercise) were common. Then pigs were housed in old railway carriages, dog kennels, cowsheds, yards and so on. In the 1930s the *Danish* or *Scandinavian piggery* came in. It was totally enclosed so that the pigs' body heat kept them warm. This reduced the feeding bill. Separate living and dunging areas were laid out. Look out for evidence of insulation and ventilation in the piggeries on any farm you visit.

Covered yards

Has the yard been covered in to protect the cattle and the manure? In the 'High Farming' period of 1820–80, scientific research for the first time affected farm building, when it showed that unprotected manure lost 50 per cent of its value. Look for *boxes* or *stalls*. These were built to ensure weaker animals got as much food as stronger ones. See if there are signs that trolleys running on tracks brought the food to them. Outside gutters and downpipes were fitted to buildings to protect stock from rainwater.

Look out for tiled and slate roofs replacing thatched ones, and bricks replacing local stone. Galvanised (coated with zinc) corrugated iron sheeting and concrete were appearing too. Cast-iron stalls and pig troughs were mass-produced. Implement and fertiliser sheds were another new feature.

Poultry

For centuries poultry ran loose in the yard but modern methods aiming at high production changed all that. Five systems need investigating:

(a) *Tiered cages* From 1918 to 1939 egg production increased and the number of hens doubled. The old egg-and-meat 'dual-purpose' bird was replaced by the egg-producer. As cod-liver oil gave them vitamin D, which they otherwise got from the sun, they could now be kept permanently indoors and no longer needed fields. A system of tiers of cages was tried. This made feeding, egg collecting and manure removal easy.

(b) *Range system* As with pigs, poultry numbers declined temporarily in the Second World War and scientific research helped afterwards. In the 1930s one-third of all eggs were imported; none were imported in the 1950s. In the late 1940s the range system – light, fixed houses or movable pens in pastures – was common. But it meant a lot of work and low yields in winter.

(c) *Intensive cagebattery system*   This system, allowing more light, produced more eggs. By 1960 one-third of all hens lived in battery cages. Perhaps you may be able to look up newspapers of that period: see if you can find any protests from animal lovers against such housing.

(d) *Deep-litter system*   The birds were given free movement in an enclosed building with artificial light. One-third lived in this way.

(e) *'Broiler' system*   This marketed 100 million birds a year by 1960. The system aimed to get the best rate of growth in the first three months of a bird's life. At a temperature of 18–21 °C in subdued light and clean air, with artificial heating and good insulation, mechanical feeding and watering, the birds lived in factory-like conditions. A *broiler house* would hold 5000–10 000 birds aged from a day to ten weeks old.

Dovecotes

Pigeons would be kept in big dovecotes by the lord of the manor in medieval times. At any one time, 500–600 birds would be in the building, but over a year 1000–2000 would pass through it. As 1000 pigeons could eat 4 tonnes of the peasants' grain a month, there was a rhyme about sowing every four grains of seed:

> One for the pigeon, one for the crow,
> One to rot and one to grow.

In earlier centuries pigeons supplied fresh meat and eggs, especially in winter.

Seventeenth-century dovecote in Avebury, Wiltshire

Stables for horses

Now examine the stables if your farm has any. Check to see if they have lofts above to store hay, and to provide roof insulation to keep the horses warm. Inside, check for wooden stall partitions, set 1.5–1.8 m apart to allow grooming space. Troughs and food racks and a *tethering ring* (for tying the horse up to) were fitted in each. Sometimes a recess held candles, combs and medicines, and a hook for the harness. Are there any signs of these features? One of four layouts could have been used: the 3–4 horse stable in which the horses face along the building; the more adaptable and better ventilated layout where they face across the building; the loose box where the untied horse can move around; and the more healthy nineteenth-century feeding stable, with a yard to allow the horses out at night.

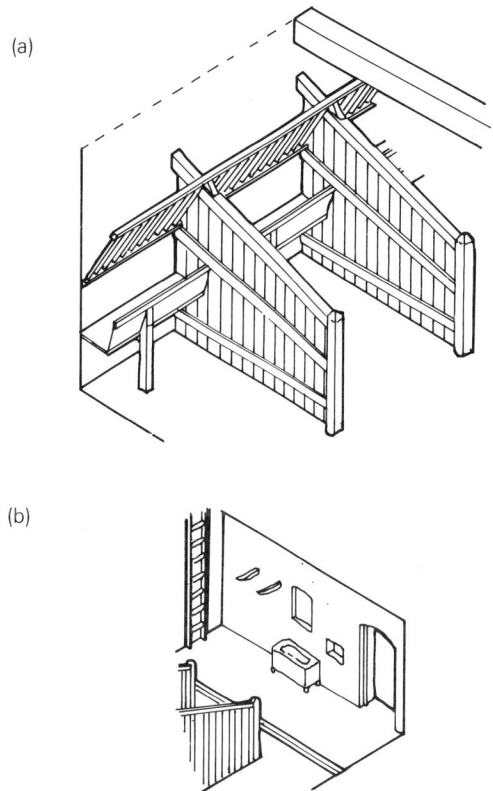

Stable interior showing (a) stalls, trough and rack, and (b) the recess, corn chest, harness hook and ladder to loft

FURTHER READING

French, M. *Farms* (Mills & Boon, On Location 10)
Harvey, N. *Old Farm Buildings* (Shire Publications, 1975)
Harvey, N. *Farms and Farming* (Shire Publications, 1977)
Peters, J. E. C. *Discovering Traditional Farm Buildings* (Shire Publications, 1986)

5 Objects from the Past

No study of the countryside would be complete without an examination of farming *artefacts*, that is man-made objects of different kinds. The countryside could not have been developed over centuries without tools and machinery. The problem is, there are so many of them that they are really a subject in their own right. Nevertheless, do try to see a collection of them in one of your local museums.

What you need to realise is that modern farming is impossible without the latest equipment, just as eighteenth-century enclosed farms depended on Jethro Tull's seed-drill and horse-drawn hoe, and medieval farming depended on the horse-drawn plough and the milking stool. When you approach farming artefacts in this way, you will be able to see more clearly why field layouts, the style and grouping of farm buildings, and changes in, for example, dairy buildings occurred in the way they did.

When you look at early ploughs, notice how the user must have held them and how their cutting edges were made. Control of such ploughs depended a great deal on the strength and skill of the user, as well as the reliability of his oxen or horses. Such a task might have been beyond the strength of many women, whereas women today can operate a tractor-pulled plough. The flail too needed a lot of stamina, since it had to be used for long hours at a time.

It is useful to divide farm machinery into two categories: things which made an important change in farming techniques, and those which simply made certain tasks easier and more comfortable to perform. The threshing machine clearly came into the first category. So why did farm labourers try to break up early threshing machines? Why were their interests different from those of the farmers who employed them? What regular task, done in the barns each winter, ended when the threshing machine came in?

Try to relate the machines and equipment you examine to their actual use down on the farm. Notice what materials the different parts of the machines are made from. Are they dangerous to use, if one is not careful? Who invented them? You may find some very interesting tales about such inventions. The *Gentlemen's Magazine*, November 1764, has a fascinating description of how Tull made his seed-drill. The 1793 edition of that magazine has an excellent description of Robert Bakewell's farm at Dishley, describing the machinery used and how all the work was done.

Besides looking at machines in museums, look for old manufacturers' catalogues in your record office or library. Not only will they illustrate the machines, but they will tell you clearly what they were capable of doing, and how much they would have cost. Fowler's Steam Ploughing Apparatus, 1856, is a good example.

Fowler's Steam Ploughing Apparatus, 1856. Notice the balanced plough (prices: three-furrow, £72; eight-furrow, £132), which can be tipped down either end for use in both directions. It did one acre in one hour, at the same cost as a horse-drawn plough, but took less time. Two 14 horsepower engines cost £1430. One hundred yards of steel rope cost £150.

If the museum has some old farming clothes, ask yourself why the *smock-frock* (an outer garment of coarse white linen) was so popular. Look particularly at footwear. Think about how well such footwear would stand up to damp, muddy conditions. When do you think farm labourers first used wellington boots? When did waterproof clothing become available, and tractors with weatherproof cabs? It is only in relatively recent times that the farm labourer has easily been able to keep really warm and dry.

Ploughing with oxen. Notice the angle of the plough handles. Why are they made like this?

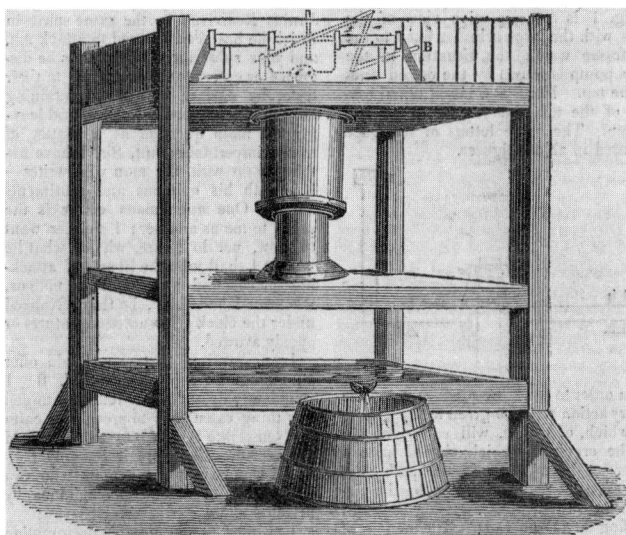

A hydraulic cider press from 1831

FURTHER READING

Bonnett, H. *Farming with Steam* (Shire Publications, 1974)

Bonnett, H. *Traction Engines* (Shire Publications, 1985)

Brigden, R. *Agricultural Hand Tools* (Shire Publications, 1983)

Ingram, A. *Shepherding Tools and Customs* (Shire Publications, 1977)

Ingram, A. *Dairying Bygones* (Shire Publications, 1977)

Major, K. *Animal-Powered Machines* (Shire Publications, 1985)

Shearman, L. R. *Portable Steam Engines* (Shire Publications, 1986)

Smith, D. J. *Discovering Horse-Drawn Farm Machinery* (Shire Publications, 1984)

Vince, J. *Discovering Carts and Wagons* (Shire Publications, 1970)

Vince, J. *Discovering Vintage Farm Machines* (Shire Publications, 1973)

Vince, J. *Discovering Old Farm Tools* (Shire Publications, 1974)

6 Talking to People

One of the most rewarding things local historians can do is to interview someone about the subject they are researching. Just as a detective thinks carefully what questions he wants answered before he sets off, so you will need to draw up a list of questions to put to your 'interviewee'. You will want to put him or her at ease at the start, so think of some good introductory questions. You may spot something on the mantelpiece, or a picture hanging on the wall, which is in some way connected with the subject you are concerned with; and so you may be able to start from there.

Do not forget to ask if he or she has a photograph album or old newspaper cuttings you can look at and discuss. If you are lucky, there may be some interesting old artefacts in the house – perhaps some harness or horse brasses, or something else connected with the subject under discussion. Looking together at such things may jog your interviewee's memory. If he or she has obviously got a lot to tell you, do not keep the interview going too long, but ask if you can come back to hear the rest. Old people can get tired, and they might think of something more to tell you by the time you return. (Incidentally, it might be a nice idea to offer to do a bit of gardening or an errand for them, in return for giving you their time. Do not forget to send them a Christmas card later on!)

You will need a portable cassette recorder. A battery-powered one is easier to handle, as you may otherwise find problems in plugging yours in. Do a short test recording to check on echo problems, etc. When you start, say whom you are interviewing and where, and give the date. This will prevent any confusion later on if you record a number of interviews. If possible, try to get the whole recording typed out on paper. Then you can edit it down to a reasonable length and cut out any repetitions. Otherwise, simply write down the most important parts of the tape. (Make sure you do not distort what the interviewees said when you select!)

Here is an example of how interesting recording oral history can be. It is an interview given to Norman Wills, a history teacher in Lincolnshire, about growing woad in the Fens. Woad is a blue dye which was used until indigo came along. The industry declined with the introduction of man-made indigo after 1878. The extract comes from Mr Wills's booklet, *Woad in the Fens*.

A tape recording of Mr Walter Booth, son of the last Skirbeck Woad Mill owner, Skirbeck, near Boston, Lincolnshire, 1971

I am Walter Booth aged 78 years. Today is the 23 January, 1971. My father, Thomas Booth, owned Skirbeck Woad Mill up to 1938, when it closed down.

I remember thatched cobs being made to keep the sheaves in. After flailing it was sown, the seed was sown, with a management drill. Manure included ground 400 tons of sprats one year on 17 acre of woad. The woad grew to 3 feet [1 m] high, was scythed, and collected up with a hay bobber.

After being weeded on the hands and knees with woad spuds it was soon ready to be plucked. Woad for seed was plucked only once. The woad was taken to the mill in carts in hessian to put over the top. The leaves were spread 4 feet [1.2 m] deep on the mill bed. After balling they took it to drying ranges and left for two months. The corners, the carriers rather, wore hats stuffed with hay. The balls were next broken up with the backs of hoes and water added, in the couch house. It was laid up to eight bricks high. The 40 tons from each couch, there being 120 tons overall, was packed into tubs of about 20 cwt [about 1000 kg], one exceptional tub weighed 35 cwt [about 1750 kg].

The tubs were taken to Boston Railway Station by a wagon termed as cuts, of which three [wagons] took three tubs. It was taken by rail to Bradford, Leeds, Buckfastleigh in Devonshire and once we exported to America.

My father was taken to Skirbeck churchyard in a woadcart in 1943.

In my early youth my father showed me some old foundations of mud huts which used to be used in those days by the labourers who worked as waddies and lived in these huts and if they left and went to work elsewhere they took the grates with them and new people coming in brought their own grates with them to put in these mud huts.

You will find quite a number of *technical terms*, that is special words connected with the woad trade, in this interview. Hopefully the interviewer knew what they meant from his earlier research. If not, he would have had to ask Mr Booth to explain them. What do you think was meant about taking old Mr Booth to the churchyard in a woadcart?

7 Putting the Evidence Together

Now that we have examined different ways of approaching local history, it will be helpful to see how a complete study can be carried out. Below are two rather different studies, different not only because the subjects are so different, but also because the research involved emphasises different types of evidence.

Case Study 1:
COLD WESTON DESERTED VILLAGE, SHROPSHIRE

This is a case study carried out by a group of 13-year-olds from Ludlow School in Shropshire, and shown on BBC TV. The Cold Weston settlement is southwest of Brown Cless Hill, and little survives of it today. Their teachers had spotted significant signs in the landscape which they felt were worth investigating.

Only a cottage which is still occupied remains, standing 100 m from the road. Nearby a deeply sunken path up the hillside passes the house. Another wider, hollowed-out track parallel to it is 100 m to the right. If this is an old road, the farmer must still be using it for his cattle as there is a gate at one end.

Pupils following this track were doubtful if it was a natural hollow, as the original ground level appeared to lie on either side. The hollow is 2 m deep. So it was probably the original entrance to a village or other site, and the path has sunk from continual use. They found further clues at the end of the path, some bumps and hollows. A closer examination showed they were roughly square or rectangular, and that they stood in line. The path continued along the side of them, and then branched out between them. Pupils then found some exposed stonework at ground level. These could be stone platforms on which timber-framed houses stood. Aerial photography was then carried out.

Ground level view of the site. What features can you pick out?

The photographs showed the earthworks spread more widely than first realised. The houses seemed to form a pattern round an open area. Could this be the village green? Although the field slopes, one large area was flatter than its surroundings. Maybe it was deliberately levelled for house building. Nearby steeply sloping ground drops to a small hollow. Was it where water was obtained? The photographs also showed four rectangular shapes which you can hardly see on the ground. They were probably Celtic fields, older than the medieval ridge and furrow fields which the photographs also revealed. The ridges and furrows could be checked on the ground quite easily.

The pupils then spotted another hollow on the photographs, and found it to the north of the village and running east–west across the fields. Here they found earthworks, and fruit trees growing. They had to be careful not to assume they had found a medieval orchard, although they might have done! Then some nettles provided a clue to human habitation, and around it the remains of a cottage complete with beams and stones. Closer examination showed bricks and an old cast-iron oven which suggested the cottage was not a medieval one. Oral history revealed the answer when the pupils questioned the local farmer. He said he had once lived in it!

An aerial photograph of the Cold Weston site

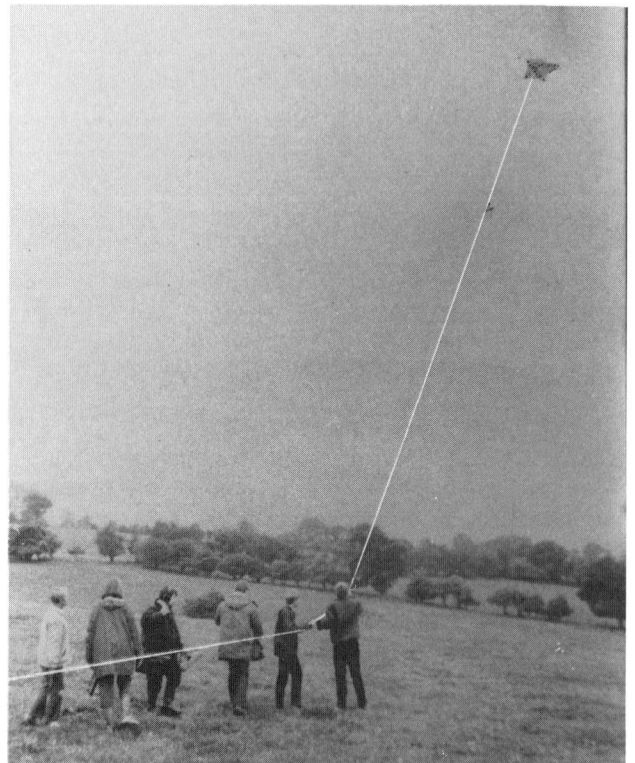

Aerial photography being carried out by Ludlow School

34

The final piece of evidence confirming this to be a deserted village was the discovery of a church behind a copse of trees. Parts of the church were Norman but it had been extended in later centuries. The churchyard was unusual as it was circular in shape. This meant it had been built in an area probably previously used for worship – perhaps even in prehistoric times.

The conclusions reached were that this site could be pre-Roman and that it was certainly a medieval village. For further evidence, they turned to documents. Pupils began by looking at *Antiquities of Shropshire*, 12 volumes by E. W. Eyton, which simply said 'the evidence regarding this Manor and Parish is so extremely inconclusive'. The fact that Cold Weston is not mentioned in the *Domesday Book* shows it was not important then, if it existed at all.

Fortunately a document mentions a watermill there in 1256, and another of 1259 mentions a land dispute. Then in 1272 the Abbot of Shrewsbury complained about Roger Tyrel owing rent there. In 1291 an *inquisition post mortem* (investigation after death) followed the death of the important landowner, Philip de Bagesover. It says he was a tenant of Lawrence de Ludlow and held 10s worth of land at Cold Weston. This suggests the village still existed but was not wealthy. In 1291 a tax survey ordered by Pope Nicholas IV recorded that the village was not worth £4, and that the Abbot got a pension of 3s a year from it.

The tax document called *Collection of the Ninth*, 1340–1, covered 27 counties and recorded that Cold Weston had at one time been valued at £4 3s, and that in 1340 it was worth only 4s 'because the chapel is in a waste place'. It recorded that its many animals had died of *murrain* (cattle disease), and there were only two tenants left. The rest had fled to avoid the tax and no priest was willing to stay there.

Thus a deserted village came alive, although it was probably always a poor place. *Reading* the landscape, and checking the archives, had produced the story.

The church at Cold Weston. What Norman features can you spot?

Case Study 2:
COLD ASTON ENCLOSURE, COTSWOLDS

At King's School, Gloucester, students looked at the archives connected with the enclosure of farmland at Cold Aston (also called Aston Blank), near Northleach on the Cotswolds. The archives are in the Gloucestershire County Record Office, and your own county record office may well have sufficient documents to do a similar study.

Letters, accounts, posters, legal documents, minutes of meetings and maps are some of the items they had to study in order to unravel what amounted to a year of revolution in this small village.

They found that the squire, who was the Bishop of Waterford in Ireland, had never lived in the village. But when his daughter married the Revd Henry Noble in

1794, the Bishop decided to rent his 717 acres (290 hectares) of strips in the open fields at £276 a year to his new son-in-law. (Henry was *not*, incidentally, the vicar of the village.) Investigation of the archives showed that the strips only produced £275 16s 8d a year. At first sight this suggested the Bishop did not approve of the marriage. In fact he and Henry had plans to increase the income from the land. They had agreed that the village's 1598 acres (647 hectares) of open fields should be enclosed.

The students discovered that nine people owned the strips in the fields. They knew from their history lessons that, provided the owners of four-fifths of the strips agreed, a private Act of Parliament could be applied for to force everyone to change the layout of the village. Instead of having strips scattered over the open fields, each owner would have a compact farm to use as he or she liked. To ensure that the fortunes of each landowner could be properly followed, several students were

Cold Aston Enclosure, Gloucestershire, 1795: State of Property for the Committee of the House of Commons

allocated to each one. This made it easier to keep an eye on the accounts, and the pre- and post-enclosure maps.

They examined the document on the previous page, which shows how many acres each owner had in 1767 and at the time of enclosure. Note, Edmund Waller is described as the 'impropriator' which means he, or his family before him, had acquired the right to the bulk of the rector's tithes. Do not confuse Noble, the squire, with James who is the vicar (parish priest). *Glebe* land meant the vicarage farm. *A. R.* and *P.* stand for *acres, rods* and *perches*, all land measurements.

It was soon clear that only a small minority of rich owners needed to be in favour of enclosure for the application to Parliament to go ahead. This was because the law stated that it was *the owners of four-fifths of the strips*, not four-fifths of the owners, who had to be in favour. The groups of students were encouraged to think what 'their' owner would gain or lose by enclosure.

One document they examined was the public notice which was put up on the church noticeboard, announcing that the Enclosure Act was being applied for.

The notice put up on Cold Aston church noticeboard on 10 August, 1794

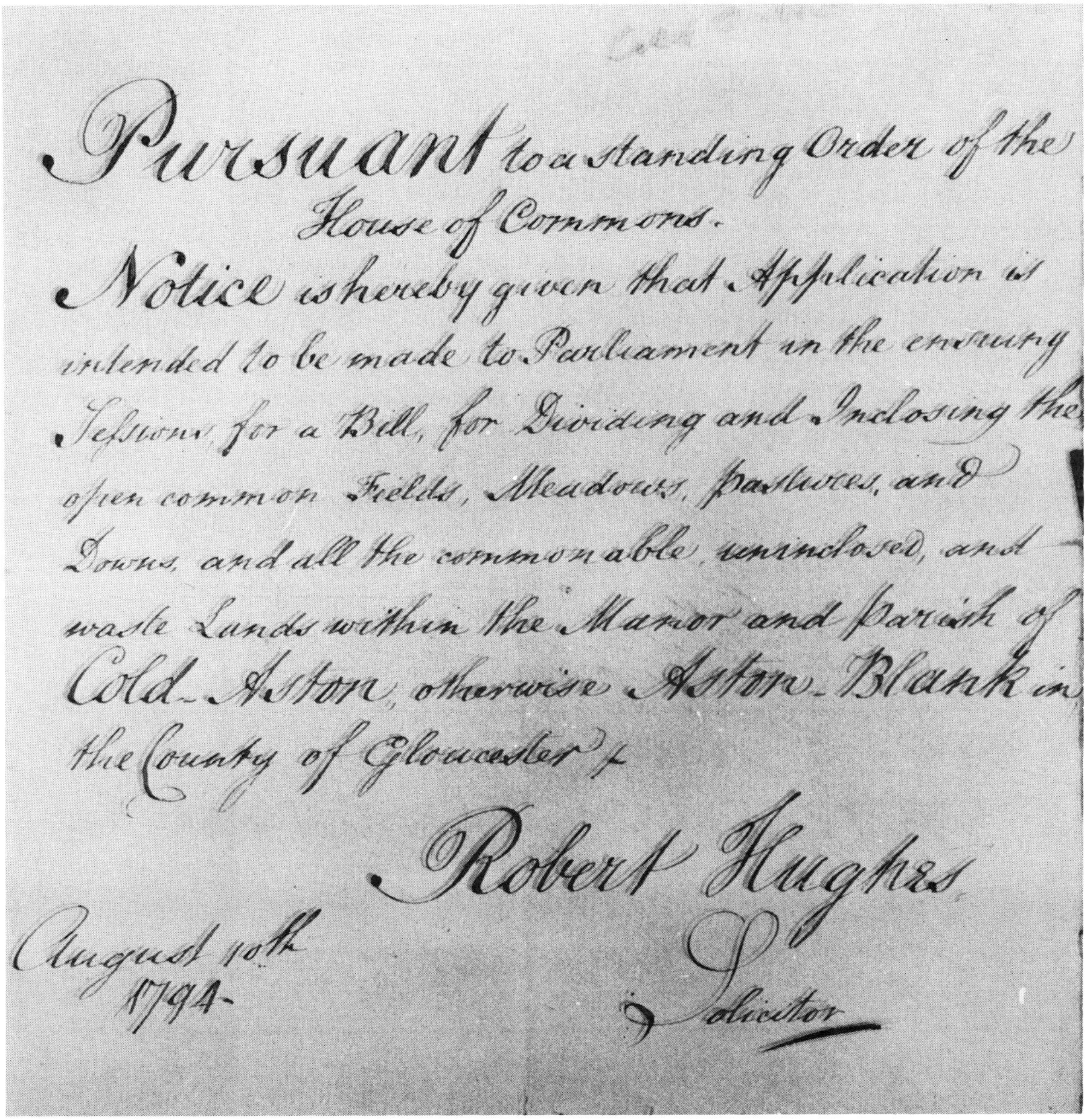

Pursuant to a Standing Order of the House of Commons.

Notice is hereby given that Application is intended to be made to Parliament in the ensuing Session, for a Bill, for Dividing and Inclosing the open common Fields, Meadows, pastures, and Downs, and all the commonable, uninclosed, and waste Lands within the Manor and parish of Cold Aston, otherwise Aston Blank in the County of Gloucester.

Robert Hughes

August 10th 1794.

Solicitor

By this time the squire had a solicitor acting for him; while another well-off owner had his own solicitor too, leaving the rest of the villagers to hire one solicitor between them all. The squire was advised that his share of the enclosure costs would be £2000. The students had to wait until they had finished looking at the archives before they could see if this was right or not.

The three solicitors were to meet frequently at a Northleach inn, to discuss how to draw up the Bill to present to Parliament, and then to decide how to allocate the land.

The Act, passed in 1795, ordered the enclosure to be done within the year and appointed the three solicitors as *commissioners* with full powers to carry it out. Students found the document containing the oath which the commissioners had to take, saying they would do the job fairly and honestly. A surveyor, Mr Clarke, was appointed to measure up all the strips and later to mark out the new farms the commissioners allocated. As the commissioners' *Minute Book* recorded, all the owners had to prove they owned their strips and say where they would like their farms to be. The Act also ordered that

some woodland was to be left so that the poor could get fuel, as well as giving the commissioners authority to build new roads if need be, and to allocate a site for quarry work to produce the necessary stone. The old freedom allowing villagers to collect fuel or to graze animals on land owned in common (*the rights of common*) was abolished. They were given power to order the growing of clover over all the farmland during the year of the changeover from open fields to enclosure; and to order the owners to hedge and ditch their land. The commissioners were entitled to payment whenever they met to carry out the Act's instructions.

The students found the Minute Book of the commissioners very useful, as it took them through the different stages of the changeover. In May 1795 the commissioners told the owners to consider new road routes, and grow clover on their strips. In July they heard objections to the road routes, then ordered the surveyor to work out the land allotment and stake out the boundaries on the ground. Mr Clarke had marked all the owners' strips on a huge map which still survives. Now he had to draw a final map showing where everyone's farm would be after enclosure. That map still exists too.

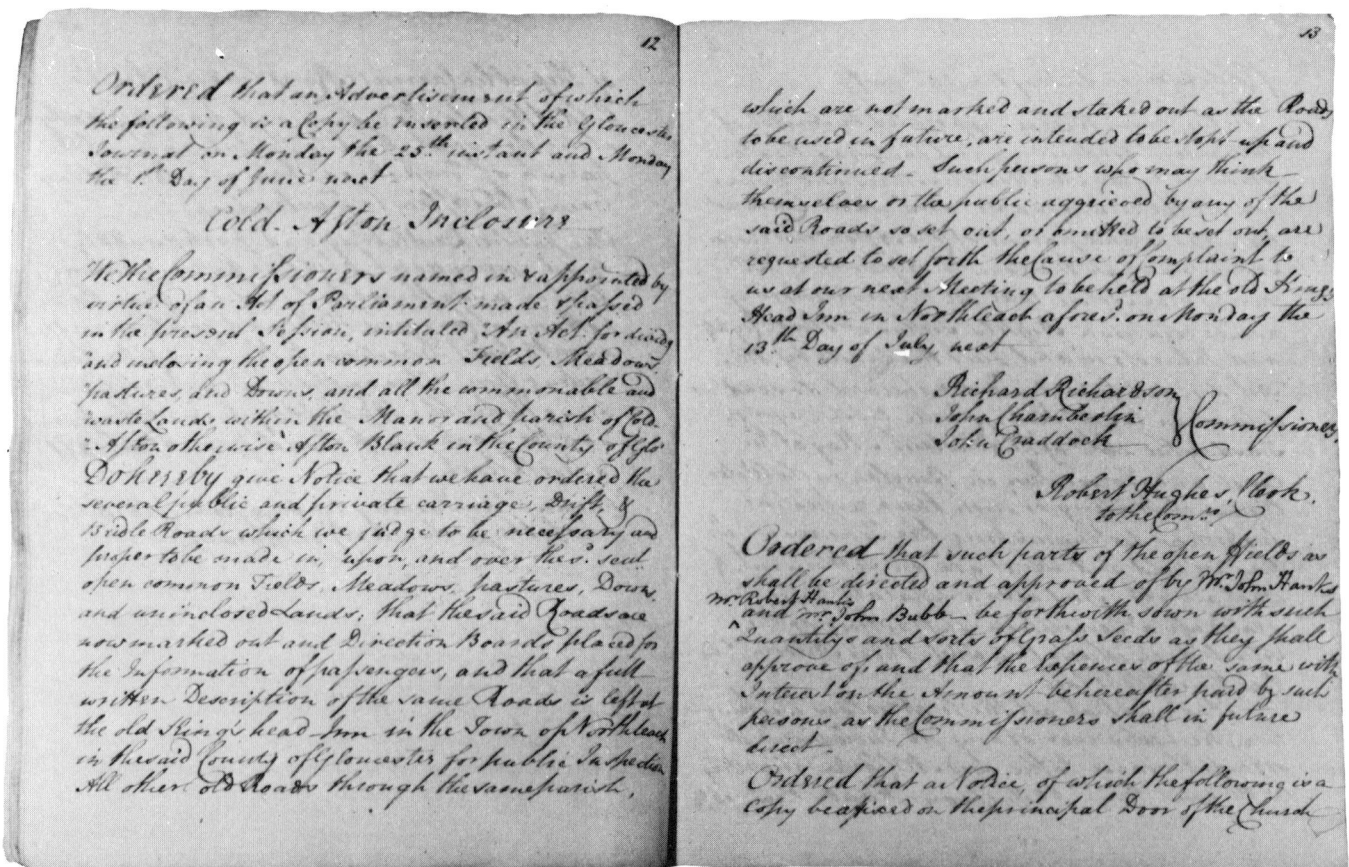

The Minute Book of the Commissioners recording their meetings at a Northleach inn shows how the business progressed.

Ways in the said Parish, which Lands shall be fenced in such Manner, and by such Person or Persons, as the said Commissioners shall by their Award order and direct.

And be it further Enacted, That the said Commissioners shall, and they are hereby authorized and required to set out, allot, and appoint unto and for the said *Mungo Henry Noble,* as Lord of the Manor of *Cold-Aston,* otherwise *Aston-Blank,* aforesaid, such Parts of the Common and Waste Lands hereby intended to be divided and inclosed, as in the Judgment of the Commissioners making the same, shall be a reasonable Satisfaction and Compensation of and for all the Right of Soil and other Manerial Rights, which he the said *Mungo Henry Noble,* as Lord of the Manor aforesaid, now hath, or might or ought to have had therein if this Act had not been passed.

Allotment to the Lord of the Manor for his Manerial Rights on the Waste Lands.

And whereas Fuel is scarce in the said Parish of *Cold-Aston,* otherwise *Aston-Blank,* and the Poor have no Wood or Furze in Common Right, the Proprietors therefore are willing and desirous of giving, towards supplying the Poor with Fuel, Part of the Lands by this Act directed to be inclosed: **Be it therefore further Enacted,** That the said Commissioners shall, and they are hereby required to set out and allot to the said *Mungo Henry Noble,* and the present Vicar and his Successors, and the Lord of the said Manor for the Time being, and the Churchwardens and Overseers of the Poor of the said Parish for the Time being, such Plot or Plots of the said Open Lands or Grounds bearing Thorns, Underwood, or Furze, as shall, in the Judgment of the said Commissioners, be of the clear Yearly Value of Fifteen Pounds at the least; and the Thorns, Underwood, and Furze arising and growing on such Plot or Plots, shall from Time to Time be distributed to the Poor of the said Parish of *Cold-Aston,* otherwise *Aston-Blank,* in such Manner and Proportions as the said Lord of the Manor, Vicar, Churchwardens and Overseers of the Poor of the said Parish for the Time being, or the major Part of them, shall think fit and determine; and if at any Time hereafter it shall appear right and proper in the Judgment of the said Lord of the Manor, Vicar, Churchwardens and Overseers, or the major Part of them, to let out to farm the said Plot or Plots of Ground, and apply the Rent thereof to purchase Fuel for the Poor, in such Case it shall be lawful for the Lord of the said Manor, Vicar, Churchwardens and Overseers of the Poor for the Time being, or the major Part of them, to let the said Plot or Plots of Ground for such Time as they shall judge
\ proper,

Allotment for Fuel to the Poor.

An extract from the Act for Dividing and Enclosing the Open Fields of Cold Aston, 1795

39

ASTON BLANK
PRE-INCLOSURE MAP 1752

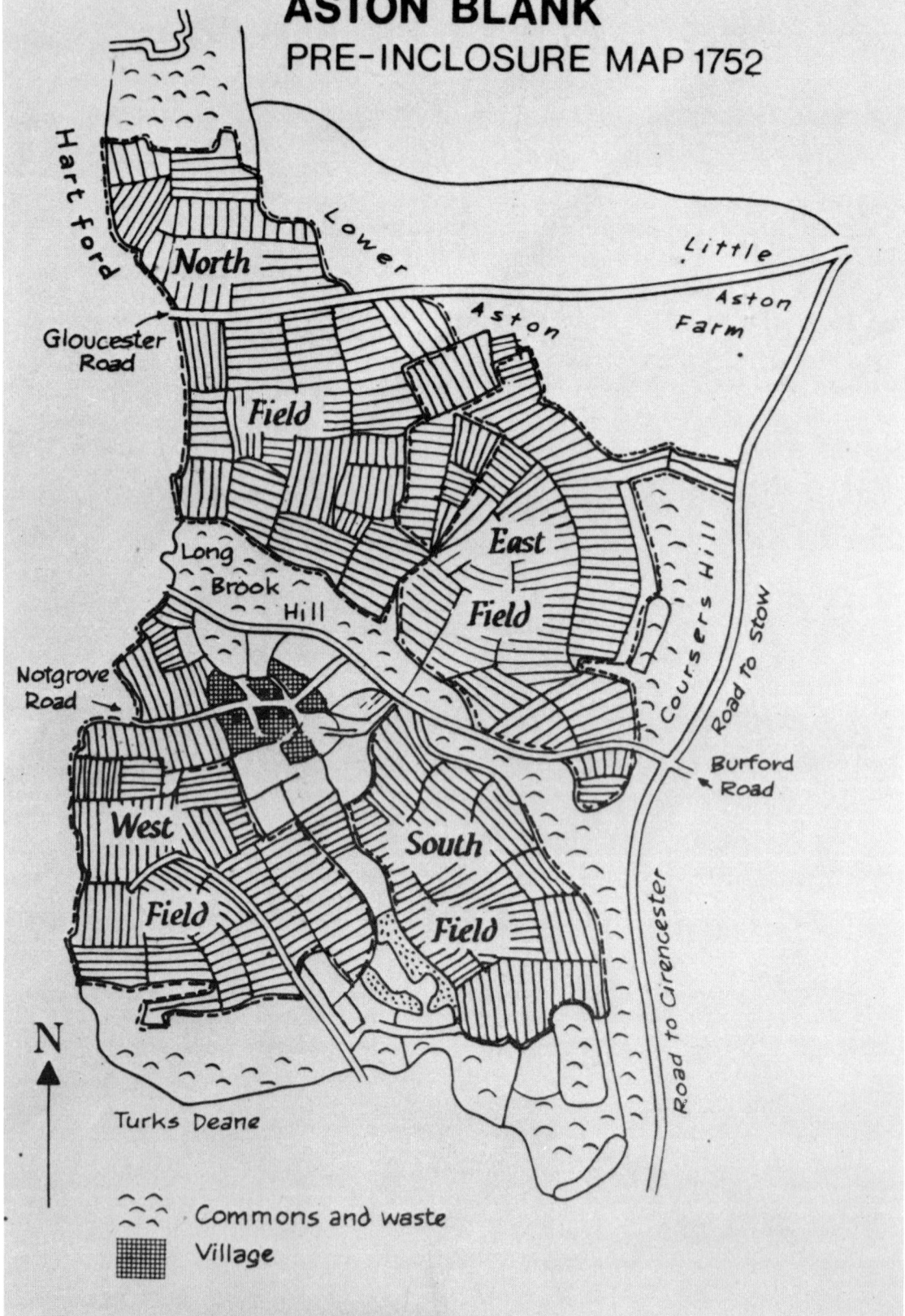

Hartford

North

Gloucester
Road

Field

Lower

Aston

Little

Aston
Farm

Long
Brook
Hill

East

Field

Coursers Hill

Road to Stow

Notgrove
Road

West

Field

South

Field

Burford
Road

Road to Cirencester

N

Turks Deane

~~~ Commons and waste

▦ Village

The simplified pre- and post-enclosure maps of Cold Aston (Aston Blank)

40

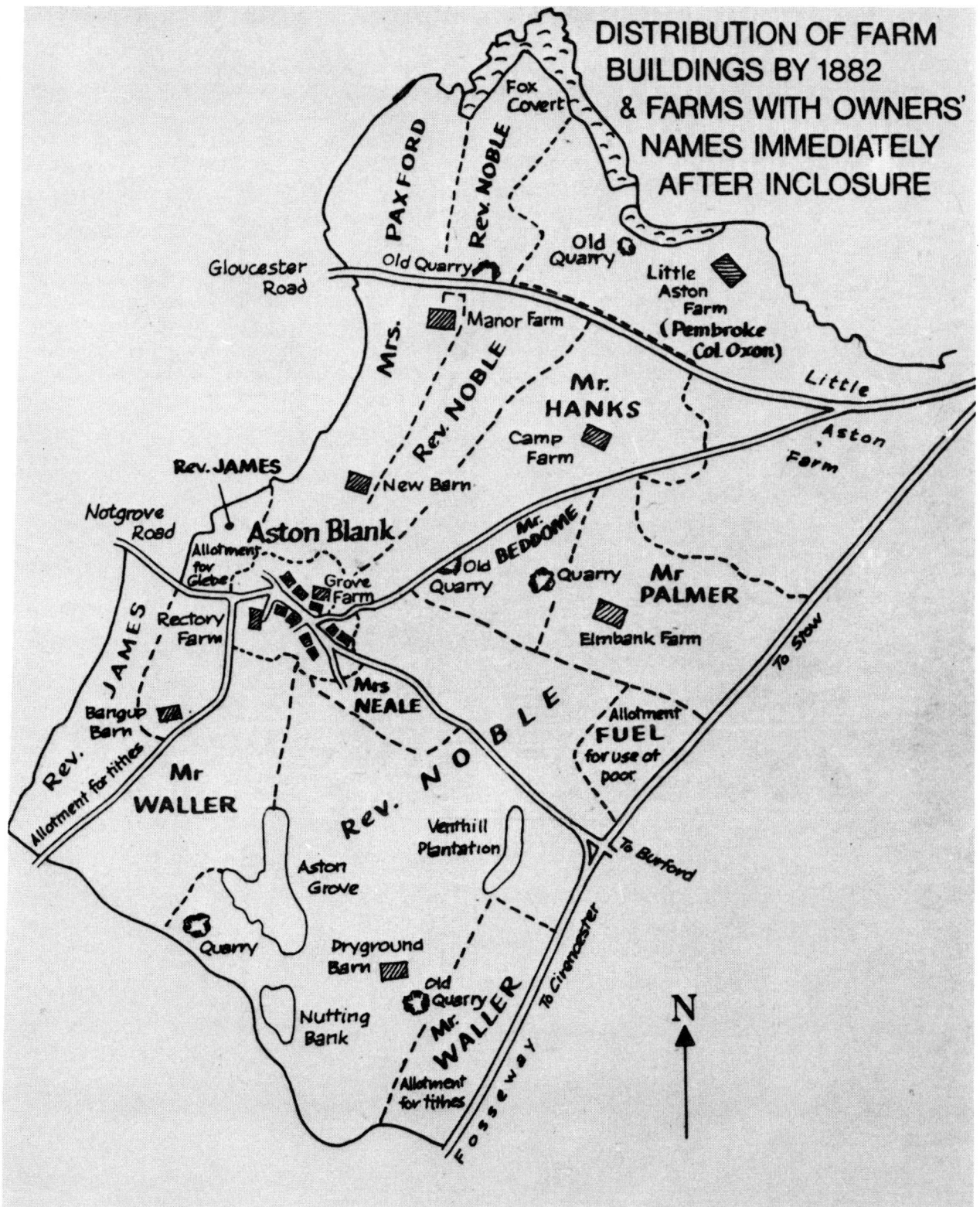

DISTRIBUTION OF FARM BUILDINGS BY 1882 & FARMS WITH OWNERS' NAMES IMMEDIATELY AFTER INCLOSURE

After examining both maps, answer these questions. How many 'on site' farmsteads have been built as a result of the enclosure? Where was fuel obtained (a) before, and (b) after, enclosure? Explain why the new roads have been routed as shown.

With the allocation of land settled, students had to examine the costs involved and see whether 'their' particular owners had done well or not. The commissioners met for the last time in January 1796. The cost of passing the Act, including Parliament's fee, the commissioners' fees, and the surveyor's maps and work came to £1140. The new roads cost £600 and the clover seed £160. The total cost had to be shared among the owners in proportion to the acreage they owned. The vicar had surrendered his glebe land (the land which went with his job) and share of the tithes, and Mr Waller had likewise given up his tithes. So they both had extra acres allocated to them. Thus the vicar got 116 acres instead of his original 36, and Mr Waller got 237 acres instead of 15.

The exciting thing was to find out whether Henry had had to pay £2000 for the changeover (as he had been advised), and whether he would now have a greater income than the rent he had to pay to his father-in-law, the Bishop of Waterford. All his accountant's calculations still exist, so it was easy to find out. He had to pay £541 1s 2d towards the passing of the Act, and the commissioners' and surveyor's fees; £48 4s for fencing, etc.; £126 19s 9d towards the roads; and £74 14s for clover seed; a total of £1121 19s 11d. But on top of this he had to pay for a lot of new farm buildings, so that in all he paid out £5800. One document shows how he was advised to sell lands he held in other villages, to pay for all this. He followed this advice. In the end he found he was able to make £852 a year from his newly enclosed farmland at Cold Aston which was organised as three separate farms.

Thus the students of King's School, by examining the archives, were able to learn a very great deal about what amounted to a revolution in the lives of the people of Cold Aston. Naturally, a trip to the village would confirm the layout of the new roads and farm boundaries.

8 Background Reading

In addition to the further reading given at the end of chapters, the following books may provide useful background information:

Addy, J. *The Agrarian Revolution* (Longman, Then and There Series, 1968)

Aston, M. *Interpreting the Landscape – Archaeology in Local Studies* (Batsford, 1985)

Creasey, J.S. *Victorian and Edwardian Country Life in Old Photographs* (Batsford, 1977)

Fowler, P. *Farms in England, Prehistoric to Present* (HMSO, 1983)

Hart, E. *The Heavy Horse* (Shire Publications, 1986)

Harvey, N. *A History of Farm Buildings in England and Wales* (David & Charles, 1982)

Herdman, M. *Hunters and Early Farmers in Britain* (Nelson, History in Evidence Series, 1985)

Jackman, L. *Exploring the Hedgerow* (Evans Bros, 1976)

Jennings, T. *The World of a Hedge* (Faber, 1978)

Muir, R. *Shell Guide to Reading the Landscape* (Michael Joseph, 1981)

Taylor, C.C. *Fields in the English Landscape* (Dent, 1975)

Toulson, S. *The Drovers* (Shire Publications, 1980)

Vince, J. *Old Farms, An Illustrated Guide* (John Murray, 1982)

Voysey, A. *Looking at the Countryside* (Routledge & Kegan Paul, Local Search Series, 1971)

Whiting, J.R.S. *Agriculture, 1730–1872* (Evans Bros, 1971)

Woodforde, J. *Farm Buildings* (Routledge & Kegan Paul, 1983)

Index